ERNANI CONTIPELLI

INTRODUCTION TO CIRCULAR ECONOMY

2024

Table of Contents

INTRODUCTION   4

1. ENVIRONMENT, SOCIETY AND ECONOMIC GROWTH   10
    1.1. A Simple Lesson   10
    1.2. Understanding Economic Growth   14
    1.3. Doughnut Economics and Planetary Boundaries   26

2. SUSTAINABLE DEVELOPMENT AND CIRCULAR ECONOMY   42
    2.1. Sustainable Development   42
    2.2. The Rise of the SDGs   50
    2.3. The Sustainable Development Beyond SDGs   56
    2.4. From Linear to Circular Economy   58
    2.4.1. Circularity and Value Creation   61
    2.4.2. Circularity and the SDGs   69

3. CIRCULAR ECONOMY: PRINCIPLES AND STRATEGIES   72
    3.1. Principles of Circular Economy   72
    3.2. Circular Strategies   87
    3.2.1. Circularity and SDG Targets   91

4. HYPER-CONSUMPTION AND CIRCULARITY: PLANNED OBSOLESCENCE   120
    4.1. Hyper-Consumption   120
    4.2. Planned Obsolescence   126
    4.2.1. Fast Fashion   130
    4.3. Sustainable Consumption and Circularity   137

4.3.1. Circular Fashion Industry	146
4.3.2. Collaborative Consumption	153
5. INNOVATION AND CIRCULAR ECONOMY	**159**
5.1. The Concept of Innovation	159
5.1.1. Creative Destruction	162
5.1.1.2. Circularity and Creative Destruction	169
5.2. Circular Innovation and Business Strategies	173
5.2.1. Business Values and Circular Strategies	175
5.2.2. Data for Circularity	179
5.3. Circular Strategies and the Entrepreneurial State	186
6. CONCLUSION	**194**
7. REFERENCES	**202**

CONTIPELLI, Ernani

Introduction to Circular Economy. Ernani Contipelli. Den Haag, Netherlands: Remote Connections for Sustainability, 2024.

ISBN: 9798337821610

1. Circular Economy. 2. Sustainability. 3. Consumption. 4. Production. Innovation. 5. Innovation.

To Gabriel and Simo.

INTRODUCTION

The world is currently facing a crisis of values, marked by the disconnection between our societal priorities and actions, which are not in harmony with the long-term well-being of our planet. It is essential for us to fully understand our reality.

Environmental degradation and social stress caused by our global production and consumption patterns are clear evidence of this crisis. These issues mainly affect the Earth's ability to regenerate and sustain the resources required for humans to thrive.

In this context, we need to address common global challenges to generate fairer and more resilient paradigms for our society. This reconstruction should be rooted in a human-centered approach, which is essential for empowering individuals, communities, and all kinds of institutions to balance economic progress, environmental protection, and social needs.

We have already initiated the debate on reshaping our paradigms, and the Circular mindset is one of the proposed approaches. It holds the potential to be applied at different social levels, offering a more sustainable lifestyle and creating new economic growth opportunities. By designing innovative business and government policy models, it can lead to a fundamental change in our prevailing values, fostering sustainability and long-term prosperity.

Despite the growing number of publications on the Circular Economy, there is still a lack of consensus on its precise concept. It is unclear whether it refers to an economic system or a development model aimed at protecting the planet and ensuring prosperity or if it is an idea that goes beyond these forms to provide a better understanding of the relationship between nature, society, and the economy.

The present study aims to provide an introductory analysis of the circular economy. It focuses on understanding its fundamental concepts from a transdisciplinary approach that considers the interconnections between various fields, particularly the public and private sectors. The study discusses the challenges and opportunities of the circular economy and describes the theories and tools that support its principles and strategies. It also relates these concepts to the contemporary debate on sustainability at both macro and micro levels.

To illustrate these objectives, we have elaborated the chapters to be easy to digest and appealing to academia and businesses interested in circular economy. They include practical examples and case studies covering diverse topics, from government development policies to companies' strategies and models. Real-life data is included to demonstrate the extent of the circular phenomenon. This diversity ensures that the research is comprehensive and provides a preliminary overview of the circular economy.

In Chapter 1, we focused on economic growth and its impact. This chapter highlights the connection between nature, society, and the economy and discusses historical and future projections related to circular challenges. We also explore the implementation of the doughnut economy, an innovative circular program that rethinks the concept of growth and prosperity at various levels of our society, from local governments to businesses.

Chapter 2 analyzes sustainable development and its triple dimension. By tracing its institutional and historical evolution from the Brundtland Report to the Agenda 2030, we understand how this evolution has shaped the current structure of the Sustainable Development Goals (SDGs). We also explore the intricate relationship between sustainability and circularity, differentiating them from the linear economic model. In this stage, a substantial part of our discussion is dedicated to analyzing the challenges and opportunities associated with the transition to the circular economy and investigating the idea of multiple value creation.

Chapter 3 underlines the foundational and interconnected principles of the circular economy - efficiency, sufficiency, and fairness. These principles are both theoretical concepts and practical strategies that can be applied in professional practices. The chapter also explores the strategies associated with these principles: elimination of waste, keeping products and materials in use, and natural system regeneration.

We contextualize these principles and strategies within the framework provided by SDG 12 and its targets, to better understand their implications. These insights are crucial for ensuring responsible production and consumption patterns by closing the loop between resources and waste through circularity.

In Chapter 4, we discuss the concepts of hyper-consumption and the various aspects of planned obsolescence. Our goal is to rethink and redefine consumption through a circular approach and align it with sustainability. By examining these relationships, we investigate the path to guide consumer behavior towards environmentally friendly, socially equitable, and economically viable use of products and services.

To illustrate these concepts more effectively, we first examine the fashion industry from the perspective of fast fashion and its adverse effects. Following this, we analyze circular fashion models, exploring their strategies and approaches.

To conclude this chapter, we present collaborative consumption as a way to advance the transition to circularity. This involves adopting mission-driven business models that seek solutions that benefit society and the environment.

Chapter 5 is focused on the relationship between innovation and circularity. It starts by exploring the concept of innovation based on Schumpeter's theory of creative destruction, situating it within today's societal challenges. Within this framework, circular innovation emerges as a disruptive approach to reshaping the roles of various stakeholders and fostering new cooperative models among them.

We examined these concepts by applying circular business strategies and their innovative approaches to value creation, as well as the theory of the entrepreneurial state and its engagement in research, strategic investments, and innovation to drive growth and progress.

As described by the structure of the chapters, the study examines the impact of circularity in various contexts, going beyond simply advocating for it and instead critically evaluating the political and social decisions needed to implement the circular transition through collaborative efforts.

Communities, entrepreneurs, consumers, and policymakers all have a role to play. They need to work together to accelerate the rise of circularity and prioritize human-centered values in our interactions as an institutional and social norm rather than an exception.

Overall, this study serves as an introduction for students, teachers, practitioners, and scholars interested in learning about circularity, its concepts, principles, and strategies. It also explores the relevance of transitioning from a linear to a circular economy and how we can progress in this direction.

Throughout the study, readers are actively engaged and invited to reflect on the meaning of circularity and how it can inspire the application of new paradigms to reshape the values of our social and economic systems in a way that respects both people and the planet.

1. ENVIRONMENT, SOCIETY AND ECONOMIC GROWTH

1.1. A Simple Lesson

Schumacher offered an insightful summary of this chapter, emphasizing its key concept by stating the following: *"through history and in virtually every part of the earth men have lived and multiplied and have created some form of culture. Always and everywhere, they have found their means of subsistence and something to spare. Civilizations have been built up, have flourished, and, in most cases, have declined and perished. This is not the place to discuss why they have perished; but we can say: there must have been some failure of resources"*[1].

In a few words, Schumacher precisely synthesized the critical problem impacting the relationship between humanity and nature: how to manage our planetary resources to allow us to thrive without compromising their ability to support livelihoods and meet our *"unlimited wants"*[2]. This issue is the

---

[1] SCHUMACHER, E. F. Schumacher, *Small is Beatiful: A Study of Economics as if People Mattered.* London: Abacus, 1990.
[2] C. McConnell and S. Brue defined *"unlimited wants"* as the *"desires of consumers to obtain and use various goods and services that provide utility – that is, pleasure or satisfaction. These wants to extend over a wide range of products, from necessities (food, shelter, clothing) to luxuries (perfumes, yachts, race, cars). Some wants – basic food, clothing, and shelter – have biological roots. Other wants – for example, the specific kind of food, clothing, and shelter we seek – are rooted in the conventions and customs of society"*. These wants change over time and tend to multiply, generating new desires and products (*Macroeconomics: Principles, Problems and Policies*, p. 22. New York: McGraw-Hill/Irwin,

primary focus of this chapter, which serves as the cornerstone for comprehending the idea of circularity.

In his book *"Collapse: How Societies Choose to Fail or Succeed"*, Jared Diamond described a possible scenario of how the society of Easter Island, the Rapa Nui, declined during the pre-colonial period. This story is a powerful example of how societies grapple with challenges arising from limited resources.

Easter Island is a small piece of land (164 km^2) and one of the most remote places in the world. It is located more than 2,300 miles away from its nearest neighbor to the west, Polynesian Pitcairn Island, and 2,300 miles off the coast of Chile to the east.

Even during pre-colonial times (around 1600), the island had dense vegetation with only a few species of plants and animals[3]. Because of its remoteness, properly managing its limited natural resources to support human settlements required significant effort.

2002).

[3] Skottsberg commented on the limited variety of native plants and animals on the island, explaining that there is no island of the size, geology, and altitude of Easter Island in the Pacific Ocean with such an impoverished flora. Nor is there an island as geographically isolated as this. The conclusion is that poverty is a result of isolation. Even considering the possibility of human involvement in the extinction of certain plant species, Rapa Nui could not have been biologically diverse (SKOTTSBERG, C. *The Natural History of Juan Fernandez and Easter Island 1*. Uppsala, Sweden: Almqvist & Wiksells Boktryckeri, 1956).

As the population grew, the demand for firewood and land for farming increased. To meet these demands, the Rapanui resorted to deforestation as a solution. Around 1000 C.E., to carve and transport their colossal stone statues, known as Moai, the inhabitants of the island cut down the giant palm trees that once dominated the island's landscape. This resulted in severe soil erosion that hindered agricultural activities.

The image below captures a collection of Moai statues located on Easter Island:

Consequently, they eventually began to overuse the resources. This led to several problems, including a reduction in the island's food supply and biodiversity, which resulted in widespread malnutrition and starvation among its inhabitants. Therefore, the Rapanui society entered a degenerative period of self-destruction, characterized by warfare, cannibalism, and population decline, ultimately culminating in their ecocide and collapse.

Of course, numerous alternative hypotheses and theories explain the collapse of Rapa Nui society. Diamond's interpretation suggests that resource scarcity plays a significant role in their fate.

The story of Rapa Nui can serve as a simple lesson for contemporary global society. Our destructive lifestyle, based on a frenetic extractive economic model, stresses the natural cycle of ecosystems and their capacity to regenerate, thus affecting our life support systems.

According to Diamond, the Rapanui are the *"clearest example of a society that destroyed itself by overexploiting its own resources"*. He continues: *"The metaphor is so obvious. Easter Island isolated in the Pacific Ocean — once the island got into trouble, there was no way they could get free. There was no other people from whom they could get help. In the same way that we on Planet Earth, if we ruin our own [world], we won't be able to get help"*[4].

The story of Easter Island serves as a cautionary tale about the consequences of mismanaging natural resources. It

---

[4] DIAMOND, J. *Collapse: How Societies choose to Fail or Succeed*, p. 118. London: Penguin Books, 2006.

demonstrates how overconsumption and environmental degradation can conduce to the collapse of a society. Today, our society confronts various resource-related challenges. By learning from the mistakes of the Rapa Nui civilization, we can take action to address these challenges and avoid a similar fate.

1.2. Understanding Economic Growth

Throughout human history, the pursuit of wealth has often been characterized by unsustainable practices as a norm, resulting in social and economic inequalities and substantial environmental deterioration. These practices have created imbalances in resource distribution and pose challenges to economic stability and environmental sustainability[5].

---

[5] In his groundbreaking book "*Capital in the Twenty-First Century*", Thomas Piketty explores the history of the capitalist economy and its role in perpetuating inequality. He argues that inequality is not a random outcome but rather an inherent characteristic of capitalist economies driven by their ideological and political systems. Piketty suggests that effective state intervention and solid policy measures are crucial to address this issue and promote a more equitable economic system, especially through the global implementation of a wealth tax (PIKETTY, T. *Capital in the Twenty-First Century*. Harvard University Press, 2020). In his most recent publication, "*Nature, Culture, and Inequality: A Comparative Historical Perspective*", he focused on environmental degradation, specifically climate change, and its interconnectedness with inequality. His argument is based on the premise that preserving planetary capacity to support human life, in the long run, is linked to simultaneously addressing the inequality challenge. He demonstrates that the richest countries aren't just the most responsible for the greenhouse gas emissions that cause climate change. The richest people in the world

Due to this process, millions of people are currently working in inhumane conditions. Our forests are being destroyed, and air, water, and soil are being polluted. These actions have led to adverse environmental and social impacts, revealing the web of interconnected issues that compromise the systems on which the future of humanity depends.

In pursuing economic growth, we take for granted the idea that our natural resources are infinite. And so, we get used to treating our planet as a sink for discarded products like carbon dioxide, plastics, and other forms of waste, which increases greenhouse gas emissions, biodiversity loss, and dependence on non-renewable resources[6].

---

emit many times the amount that the poorest do. The top 10 percent of the wealthiest people in the world account for almost half of global emissions, and the top 1 percent account for just under 17 percent of global emissions (*World Inequality Report*, 2019). Thomas Piketty's research demonstrates that the environment, inequality, and economy are interrelated and should be addressed together through holistic approaches. These approaches should prioritize human values, respect the regenerative capacity of our ecosystems, reduce wealth concentration, and promote a more equitable distribution of resources (PIKETTY, T. *Nature, Culture, and Inequality: A Comparative Historical Perspective.* New York: Other Press, 2024).

[6] Nowadays, people everywhere on our planet are interconnected to each other through the air they breathe, the climate they depend upon, the food they eat, and the water they drink. Although our wasteful lifestyles are submitting our planet's ecosystem to continuous human assault which affect the availability of renewable natural resources to meet the basic needs of present and future generations (CHESHIRE, D. *The Handbook to Building a Circular Economy*. RIBA Publishing, 2021)

One of the fundamental concepts of economics is resource scarcity, which means that we have less resources than we would like. In other words, we can only acquire some of the goods and services we desire using the available resources while we remain unsatisfied with our basic needs, such as air, water, food, clothing, and shelter. However, we require more resources to maintain our current standard of living and fulfill the "*unlimited wants*" driven by the dynamics of our current capitalist economic system[7].

Therefore, we exceed the capacity of our scarce resources, meaning people are constantly forced to choose from the limited options nature provides. Additionally, choosing to have more of one thing means having less of something else[8].

---

[7] Paul Mason discusses the characteristics of capitalism, arguing that it is more than just an economic structure or a set of laws and institutions. He believes it represents a whole system - social, economic, demographic, cultural, and ideological - necessary for a developed society to function through markets and private ownership. As a system, we can identify a number of its fundamental features. It is an organism with a lifecycle, operating beyond the control of individuals, governments, and even superpowers. It is a learning organism that constantly adapts, morphs, and mutates in response to danger, creating patterns and structures barely recognizable to the generation that came before. In short, capitalism is a complex, adaptive system that has reached the limits of its capacity to adapt (MASON, P. *Postcapitalism: A Guide to Our Future*, p. xiii. New York: Farrar, Straus and Giroux, 2016). According to the concept of circularity, capitalism can be influenced by a different set of values that can impact its adaptive system and steer it towards a more humanistic approach, oriented towards a new environmentally friendly and socially conscious mindset. This can be understood as postcapitalism, as proposed by Mason, or even conscious capitalism, or simply a new historical adaptation of the old capitalist system.

In resource scarcity, the idea of opportunity cost becomes relevant. It refers to the total cost of making a particular decision and guides us to choose the best option from all available options. According to this concept, our choices represent the value of the next best alternative that we must give up when we make a decision.

To get more than one thing, we prioritize specific actions and forgo the opportunity to get something else. This decision involves considering our values and weighing our decisions within a range of possibilities.

Currently, the opportunity cost of our contemporary economic growth model is impacting the ability of natural ecosystems to regenerate, jeopardizing the capacity of the planet to support the development of human life. Would this be rational or logical?

It is important to remember that everything we produce to meet our needs relies on our natural systems. Therefore, prosperity is not something given; instead, it depends on human interactions with the environment. These interactions determine how we extract goods and provide the services we need to sustain the "*unlimited wants*" of our society.

---

[8] BAUMOL, W. J. and BLINDER, A. S. *Economics: Principles and Policy*, p. 04. Thomson South-Western, 2003.

Of course, these interactions involve values and decisions. Choices must be made rationally, considering the opportunity costs in terms of the environmental and social impacts of our economic systems, rather than focusing solely on a race to achieve financial growth through uncontrolled resource consumption.

Ensuring the sustainable management of natural resources is crucial for humanity's overall well-being. Our current demands on the planet exceed its capacity to support us without undermining its ability to regenerate itself. These externalities demonstrate the inefficiency of our economic system in effectively managing and preserving our limited natural resources. Some estimates suggest that maintaining our current living standard would require 1.6 planets.

In his Nobel Prize-winning book *"The Climate Casino: Risk, Uncertainty, and Economics for a Warming World"*, William Nordhaus examines global warming and climate change and demonstrates how economic growth is connected to environmental degradation. According to him, the main problem is that the people who produce emissions don't pay for the harm they cause, and those who are affected don't get compensated. When we buy things, we pay for making them, but one important cost is not covered: the damage caused to the environment. These costs are considered externalities because they're not part of the market's transactions[9].

Humanity's attained prosperity has come at a high cost to the environment and its natural replenishment cycles. The economic success of any enterprise is often based on its ability to maximize profits. In these imbalanced and degenerative processes, contemporary methods of producing and consuming goods and services have become disconnected from nature and people. As a result, economic values have taken precedence over environmental and social values focused on well-being.

The question about profit maximization involves the logic of value creation within our economic system, which is primarily based on monetization. This means that value is typically expressed in financial terms[10].

---

[9] Nordhaus continues his analysis of global warming by stating that two main factors make it a significant issue. First, it is a global externality caused by people all over the world in their daily use of fossil fuels and other activities that impact the climate for decades and even centuries into the future. Dealing with global externalities like this is difficult because there is no effective market or government system in place to address them. There is no world government that can require everyone around the globe to participate in the solution. This situation presents a significant challenge for policymakers who want to slow the pace of climate change and its environmental impact to prevent its dangers for present and future generations (NORDHAUS, W. *The Climate Casino: Risk, Uncertainty, and Economics for a Warming World*, p. 18/19. New Haven: Yale University Press, 2013).

[10] Consider the logic of value centered only on wealth generation, the standard economic indicator, Gross Domestic Product (GDP), measures the progress of Nations based on a limited aspect of the economy: marketed activity to maximize production and consumption. However,

To shift towards an economic system that considers nature and people, we must reevaluate how we create value[11]. Rather than focusing on a single value, we should consider multiple values simultaneously to tackle societal and environmental challenges[12].

In simpler terms, humans' interactions with nature significantly influence the global economy. These actions can have destructive consequences on the Earth's ability to

---

the GDP overlooks many components that enhance welfare, such as non-monetary transactions and income distribution among individuals, which significantly impact well-being. Clair Brown points out that GDP has limitations because it only uses income to measure economic growth. This makes income the primary focus for countries. She believes this encourages individuals to prioritize what they buy while the country pays little attention to inequality and sustainability (BROWN, C. *Buddhist Economics: An Enlightened Approach to the Dismal Science*, p. 107. New York: Bloomsbury, 2017).

[11] See chapter 3.1. *Circularity and Value Creation*.

[12] According to Kubiszewski et al., a more comprehensive and inclusive indicator would consolidate economic, environmental, and social elements into a common framework to demonstrate net progress in improving genuine human well-being. They propose the Genuine Progress Indicator (GPI) as an alternative measure of welfare produced by economic activities. This multi-dimensional indicator draws attention to environmental protection, full employment, social equity, improved product quality and durability, and more efficient resource use, thereby capturing a wide range of factors that contribute to sustainable well-being. (KUBISZEWSKI et al. *Beyond GDP: Measuring and Achieving Global Genuine Progress*. In: Ecological Economics 93, 57–68, 2013). Another example is the application of the Gross National Happiness (GNH) Index by Bhutan. The GNH approach to development includes nine areas: psychological well-being, use of time, community vitality, cultural diversity, ecological resilience, the standard of living, health, education, and good governance, all in a balanced and holistic manner. It emphasizes the importance of collective happiness and integrates it directly into public policies, making happiness an explicit criterion in various projects and programs.

sustain its diverse ecosystems and provide the necessary resources for human life to thrive.

Considering this idea, Paul Hawken affirmed that we may have already surpassed the point at which the planet can sustainably support the world's population using the present production and consumption standards. This disturbing possibility should impel us to seek, as sensibly and quickly as possible, an integration of our wants and needs as expressed and served by commerce, with the capacity of the earth, water, forests, and fields to meet them[13].

We must convert our production processes and consumption behaviors into a system that is socially and environmentally responsible.

Wealth creation should follow a cyclical system in which restoring the environment, promoting social inclusion, and making money are the same process and part of an integrated web. Otherwise, if we continue our current collision course, in which we are moving quickly, our society will face severe disruptions.

We have embraced the linear "*take-make-discard*" approach as our economic growth paradigm, where raw materials are collected, processed, used, and disposed of,

---

[13] HAWKEN, P. *The Ecology of Commerce: A Declaration of Sustainability*, p. 309. Harper Collins Publishers, 1994.

causing excessive waste and overconsumption of our natural resources[14].

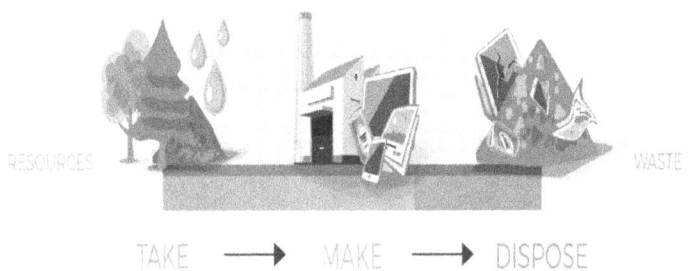

[15]

Our modern lifestyles lead us to dump waste and pollution at every stage of our productive and consumption interactions, thereby destroying the natural systems we

---

[14] The Circular Economy Glossary, published by the Ellen MacArthur Foundation, defines a linear economy as "*An economy in which finite resources are extracted to make products that are used—generally not to their full potential—and then thrown away ('take-make-waste'). It is a wasteful and polluting system that degrades natural systems*" (Available at: https://www.ellenmacarthurfoundation.org/topics/circular-economy-introduction/glossary). This definition clearly emphasizes the importance of maintaining high value for products, components, and materials over time, while also reducing environmental impact by cutting waste and other environmental stress processes such as emissions of greenhouse gases and pollution, in order to respect the limits of our planet.
[15] Available at: https://www.rit.edu/sustainabilityinstitute/blog/what-circular-economy.

depend on. As Catherine Weetman has pointed out, our economic system is shockingly wasteful. Annually, we extract a staggering 90 billion tons of natural resources to make what we consume. That's more than 12 tons for every person on the planet. If we continue at this pace, that number is likely to double by 2050[16].

In this model, waste is not only considered to be the driving force of the economic process but is seen as inevitable and acceptable in shaping its notion of value.

Moreover, the environment is perceived as a simple and cost-free source of income rather than the fundamental capital that supports and sustains our society on this planet. This viewpoint has the potential to significantly impact human life and the overall well-being of our planet.

Given that it is impossible to run a linear system indefinitely on a finite planet, society is tasked with the challenge of finding and implementing alternative patterns of living that decouple economic growth from indiscriminate consumption of natural resources through innovative processes in multiple and complex collective actions.

It's important to recognize the distinction between economic and physical growth to understand the dimension of the necessary changes and the corresponding strategies.

---

[16] WEETMAN, C. *A Circular Economy Handbook: How to Build a More Resilient, Competitive and Sustainable Business*. Kogan Page, 2020.

Economic growth refers to the sum of all final goods and services produced and their correlative values added and generated within a country during a specific period. On the other hand, the physical growth of the economy involves an increase in material and energy resources, often leading to more significant environmental impacts, degradation, and depletion of natural resources.

Paul Ekins argued that economic growth based on multiple values can be decoupled from physical growth through a process of resource consumption and environmental impacts that effectively respect our planetary boundaries. He stated, "*It is clear from experience that the relationship between the economy's value and its physical scale is variable and that it is possible to reduce the material intensity of GNP. This establishes the theoretical possibility of GNP growing indefinitely in a finite material world*".[17]

In 2011, the report "*Decoupling Natural Resource Use and Environmental Impacts from Economic Growth*", elaborated by the UN Environment Programme, revealed that

---

[17] EKINS, P. *Economic Growth and Environmental Sustainability: the Prospects for Green Growth*, Routledge, London/New York, 2000. The World Bank has already demonstrated a clear link between economic growth, waste generation, and greenhouse gas emissions. As a result, our economic progress is linked to environmental degradation, biodiversity loss, and global warming. (KAZA, S.; YAO, L.; BHADA-TATA, P.; VAN WOERDEN, F. *What a Waste 2.0: A Global Snapshot of Solid Waste Management to 2050*. Urban Development. Washington, DC: World Bank, 2018).

the global consumption of minerals, ores, fossil fuels, and biomass could triple between today and 2050 unless we find a way to decouple economic growth from the rate of natural resource consumption[18].

Therefore, decoupling economic growth rates from the amounts of consumption of the finite material world and their consequent environmental effects will demand a radical shift in behavior. This shift towards a more sustainable and dematerialized global economy is not just a challenge but also an opportunity.

To achieve sustainability, we must rethink our public policies, corporate schemes, and production and consumption patterns through multiple innovation methods, from technological breakthroughs to new business models.

Gallopin discusses the challenges of achieving sustainable development in relation to economic growth, outlining two primary scenarios for long-term sustainability. The first scenario focuses on improving people's quality of life without increasing material consumption, emphasizing growth independent of resource use, achieved through advancements in education, healthcare, and cultural experiences. The second scenario involves zero-growth

---

[18] FISCHER-KOWALSKI, M. et al., '*Decoupling Natural Resource Use and Environmental Impacts from Economic Growth*', UNEP, Available at: www.unep.org/resourcepanel/decoupling/files/pdf/decoupling_report_english.pdf., 2011.

economies, where economic output does not increase. Here, the priority shifts to environmental protection and social well-being.

Gallopin emphasizes that sustainable development does not mean stopping all economic growth; societies can maintain a zero-growth approach regarding material resources while still enhancing non-material aspects of life. This allows societies to thrive by valuing cultural achievements, psychological resilience, and spiritual fulfillment. While demographic pressures and economic growth must stabilize for ecological sustainability, cultural and spiritual growth can continue indefinitely, enabling societies to adapt without depleting natural resources[19].

Global society needs to recognize itself as part of nature and align its actions with a sustainable path to manage the Earth's resources effectively. This requires significant changes in our way of life, embracing social innovation to drive progress and reduce vulnerability for both people and the environment[20].

---

[19] GALLOPIN, G. A *Systems Approach to Sustainability and Sustainable Development*, p. 27. Economic Commission for Latin America, Santiago, 2003.

[20] According to the Stanford Graduate School of Business, social innovation can be defined as *"the process of developing and deploying effective solutions to challenging and often systemic social and environmental issues in support of social progress. Social innovation is not the prerogative or privilege of any organizational form or legal structure. Solutions often require the active collaboration of constituents across government, business, and the non-profit world"* (Sarah A.

It is possible to argue that our survival depends on the environment, and the concept of sustainability illustrates how humans and nature can interact harmoniously. With their aim to balance society, the economy, and the environment, sustainable development and circularity are keys tools in meeting the needs of present and future generations. It is through the proper management of natural resources that we can ensure the protection of our species and the planet.

1.3. Doughnut Economics and Planetary Boundaries

From an economic perspective, circular programs have the potential to reshape how our society operates by adopting innovative methods[21], such as the so-called "*Doughnut Economics*". This development model envisions a world where people and the planet can thrive in balance,

---

SOULE, S. A., MALHORTRA, N. and CLAVIER, B., *Defining Social Innovation*, Stanford GSB, Available at: https://www.gsb.stanford.edu/experience/about/centers-institutes/defining-social-innovation).

[21] Especially after the 2008 global financial crisis, there was much scholarly discussion and publications about new paradigms to move our economic system toward sustainability. For example, Coyle presents us with the Economics of Enough, which aims to raise awareness about our future challenges if we sustain the current production and consumption patterns. To change this situation, she highlights the following steps: to define prosperity beyond the GDP; to harmonize economic policies with environmental and social objectives; and to reform our institutions and their decision-making processes to promote a positive impact on sustainability and mitigate negatives such as hyper-consumption (COYLE, D. The Economics of Enough: *How to Run the Economy as If the Future Matters*. Princeton University Press, 2011).

reimagining and recreating local and global futures based on principles of circularity.

The Doughnut Economics presents a paradigm that advocates for a circular economy. It aims to rethink the traditional idea of growth and prosperity, establishing a path that brings about the regenerative and distributive dynamics appropriate for the unique context and challenges of the 21st century. In other words, it offers a framework for thinking like a 21st-century economist to bring the world's economies into a safe and just space for humanity[22].

The Doughnut's essence consists of two concentric rings. The inner ring represents a social foundation to ensure everyone can access life's essentials, including food, water, gender equality, and a political voice.

The outer ring represents an ecological ceiling to prevent humanity from exceeding the planetary boundaries that protect Earth's life-supporting systems. Between these two sets of boundaries lies a doughnut-shaped space that is ecologically safe and socially just. In this space, it is possible

---

[22] Kate Raworth, creator of the Doughnut Economics model, explains the importance of adopting this developmental approach. She argues that our current multifaceted crisis, which encompasses climate change, ecological degradation, and severe social inequalities regarding power and opportunities, requires a profound transformation of our global economic system. This transformation must prioritize regenerative and distributive aspects, ensuring that it meets the needs of all people while operating within the means of the living planet (RAWORTH, K. *Doughnut Economics: Seven Ways to Think Like a 21st-Century Economist*. London: Penguin Books, 2022).

to meet the needs of all people within the limits of our planet's natural resources, and humanity can thrive[23].

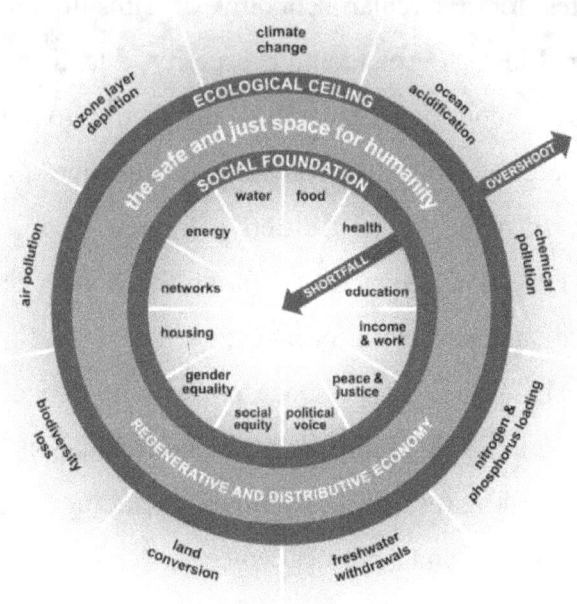

According to this system, critical human deprivation lies in the center of the hole (below the social foundation)[25], representing those who fail to meet minimum standards for

---

[23] Doughnuts Economics Action Lab. *What is the Doughnut?* Available at: https://doughnuteconomics.org/tools-and-stories/11.
[24] Doughnuts Economics Action Lab. *Doughnuts Economics Model*. Available at: https://doughnuteconomics.org/about-doughnut-economics.
[25] The 12 dimensions of the social foundation are derived from the social priorities agreed in the Sustainable Development Goals: water, food, health, education, income and work, peace and justice, political voice, social equity, gender equality, housing, networks, and energy.

income, education, healthcare, housing, food, and access to clean water and air.

The solid part of the doughnut represents the people who have access to essential resources for a good quality of life and utilize them without causing adverse environmental impacts.

The external crust lies in critical environmental degradation (beyond the ecological ceiling)[26], revealing the limits of our planet's ability to provide the essential elements to support human life. Suppose we cross the ecological ceiling, overconsuming the finite natural resources available. In that case, we will negatively affect the so-called Earth system, including climate, oceans, biodiversity, and various other planetary boundaries.

The Earth system is a complex web of interconnected processes that sustain life on our planet. It comprises various components, including the atmosphere, hydrosphere, lithosphere, and biosphere.

These components work harmoniously to create a delicate balance. The atmosphere regulates climate and

---

[26] The 9 dimensions of the ecological ceiling are the nine planetary boundaries defined by Earth-system scientists: stratospheric ozone depletion, loss of biosphere integrity (biodiversity loss and extinctions), chemical pollution and the release of novel entities, climate Change, ocean acidification, freshwater consumption and the global hydrological cycle, land system change, nitrogen and phosphorus flows to the biosphere and oceans, atmospheric aerosol loading.

weather patterns; the hydrosphere comprises oceans, rivers, and glaciers; the lithosphere encompasses rocks, landforms, and the Earth's interior; and the biosphere includes all living organisms. Together, they create a dynamic equilibrium necessary for the survival of countless species.

Change is a constant in the Earth system. It can be caused by natural factors such as volcanic eruptions and earthquakes or human activities like deforestation, pollution, overpopulation, and climate change.

However, the accelerated changes the Earth system faces today are primarily a consequence of human actions rather than solely a result of natural events during the early stages of Earth's geological history[27].

Scientific evidence clearly points to humanity's dominance over the planet, leading to the entry into the "*Age of Humans*". This marks a new chapter in the Earth's geological history known as the Anthropocene, defined by the enduring, human-driven changes to the Earth's surface. Once made, whether physical, chemical, or biological

---

[27] The difference between human and geological time is one reason why human history, geological history, and humanity and nature have usually been studied and described separately. There is also a difference in the scale of events. We now know that the Earth has changed significantly over its vast history. Until recently, mainstream geological opinion considered human influences a microscopically brief and trivial interlude in the Earth's history.

alterations, they leave indelible and lasting marks that impact the present and will shape the future of our society[28].

The role of humanity as an active agent of change in Earth's biogeochemical and biological systems marked the conclusion of the Holocene epoch and the commencement of the Anthropocene[29]. This new era is characterized by rapid and unpredictable changes occurring at rates and in directions not previously observed in human history,

---

[28] We can demonstrate the existence of the Anthropocene by examining how human activities are causing long-lasting environmental changes with irreversible and unpredictable effects on a human timescale. For instance, our current urban development can be compared to an "event layer" in geological terms, providing valuable information for future geologists studying the Anthropocene. The Earth's geological history indicates that large amounts of carbon dioxide released into the atmosphere take about 100,000 years to return to normal levels, impacting temperature, ocean acidity, and sea level. This is due to processes such as neutralization with surface rocks and carbon sequestration through increased plant growth and the burial of organic matter. Furthermore, biological changes are typically permanent, as newly introduced species and those that replace extinct organisms will continue to evolve and shape the future animal and fossil populations. These changes caused by human activity will significantly alter the Earth's history, creating a future vastly different from what we know today (ZALASIEWICZ, J. *The Human Dimension in Geological Time*. In: MÖLLERS et all. *Welcome to the Anthropocene: The Earth in Our Hands*. Munich: Rachel Carson Center, 2014).

[29] The Anthropocene would begin after the Holocene, which started approximately 11,700 years ago as the planet warmed following its last glacial period, creating the conditions necessary for the development of human life within the Earth system. In 1995, Paul Crutzen coined the term Anthropocene. He initially suggested that it began around 1800 CE, during the Industrial Revolution, when the human population and carbon-based energy use accelerated, and this period also marked the beginning of the rise in carbon dioxide levels in the Earth system. These physical markers are crucial because, in geology, we don't just consider time but also the physical evidence of time.

generating far-reaching implications for the planet and its inhabitants[30].

In the Anthropocene era, the social-ecological systems that comprise the Earth System must be resilient to effectively cope with and adapt to dynamically changing conditions while ensuring that their trajectory remains within the planetary boundaries[31].

The Planetary Boundaries framework aims to balance the development of human societies with the maintenance of the Earth System in a resilient and accommodating state. It is

---

[30] When analyzing the Anthropocene, Erle Ellis delivers a strong message about how humanity needs to approach this new geological epoch: "*It is no longer Mother Nature who will care for us, but us who must care for her (...) Clearly it is possible to look all we have created and see only what we have destroyed. But that, in my view, would be our mistake. We most certainly can create a better Anthropocene. The first step will be in our minds. The Holocene has gone. In the Anthropocene we are the creators, engineers and permanent global stweards of sustainable human nature*" (ELLIS, E. *A World of Our Making*. New Scientist 210 (2816): 26-27, 2011).

[31] BRIDGEWATER, P., KIM, R. and BOSSELMANN, K. *Ecological Integrity: A Relevant Concept for International Environmental Law in the Anthropocene?* Yearbook of international Environmental Law, Vol. 25, No. 1, pp. 61–78, 2015. To address the challenges of the Anthropocene and contain human activity within planetary boundaries, Frank Biermann introduces the concept of earth system governance as "*the interrelated and increasingly integrated system of formal and informal rules, rule-making systems, and actor-networks at all levels of human society (from local to global) that are set up to steer societies towards preventing, mitigating, and adapting to global and local environmental change and, in particular, earth system transformation, within the normative context of sustainable development*" (BIERMANN, F. *'Earth System Governance' as a Crosscutting Theme of Global Change Research*. Global Environmental Change. Human and Policy Dimensions, pp. 17, 326–337, 2007).

based on scientific analysis of the risks posed by anthropogenic destabilizations on a global scale. Therefore, it proposes boundaries for human impacts on critical Earth-system processes.

The safe operating space for global societal development defined by the Planetary Boundaries framework is based on the biophysical processes that regulate the stability of the Earth system. It aims to steer humanity away from a trajectory that could lead, with an uncomfortably high probability, to a different state of the Earth System that would be less hospitable to supporting human societies.

In other words, planetary boundaries establish clear limits for preserving ecological conditions. They define the environmental target corridor within the larger context of sustainable development or the biophysical preconditions for sustainable development[32]. This corridor encompasses the natural conditions to maintain long-term ecological balance and human well-being.

The Stockholm Resilience Centre recently published unedited research that assesses all nine planetary boundaries for the first time.

---

[32] KIM, R. and BOSSELMANN, K. *Operationalizing Sustainable Development: Ecological Integrity as a Grundnorm of International Law*. Review of European, Comparative and International Environmental Law, July 2015, DOI: 10Æ1111ØreelÆ12109

According to this research, human activities have pushed the stability and resilience of the Earth system further away from its safe operational space as we have already transgressed six of the nine planetary boundaries.

The illustration below visually represents the updated conditions of the Planetary Boundaries:

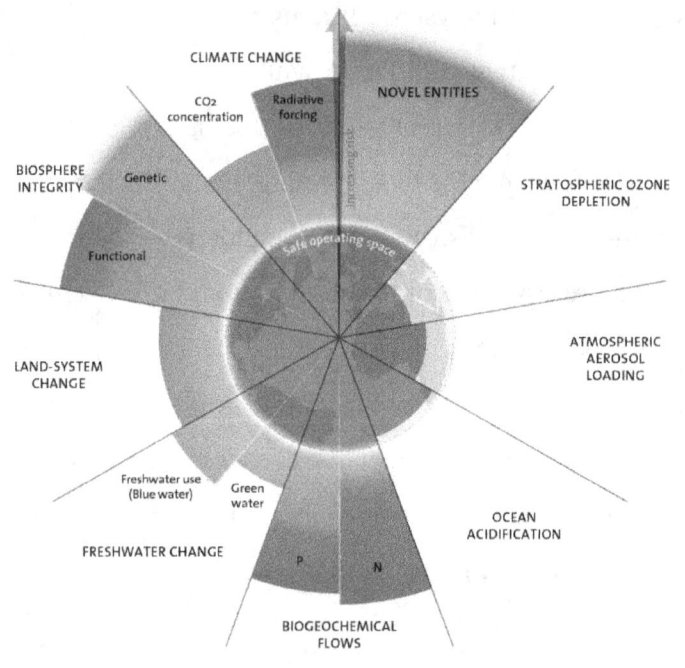

One of the leading co-authors of this study, Johan Rockström, commented: *"This update on planetary*

---

[33] The 2023 update to the Planetary Boundaries. Licensed under CC BY-NC-ND 3.0. Credit: "Azote for Stockholm Resilience Centre, based on analysis in Richardson et al 2023".

boundaries clearly depicts a patient that is unwell, as pressure on the planet increases and vital boundaries are being breached. We don't know how long we can keep transgressing these key boundaries before combined pressures lead to irreversible change and harm"[34].

The concept of planetary boundaries contributes to a better understanding of the relationship between humans and the planet and how to monitor the significant pressures caused by different anthropogenic interventions on our ecosystems. This understanding is crucial for engaging with multiple and strategic stakeholders such as policymakers, businesses, and society as a whole, in order to protect, recover and rebuild the stability and resilience of the Earth system.

---

[34] STOCKHOLM RESILIENCE CENTRE. *All planetary boundaries mapped out for the first time, six of nine crossed*. Available at: https://www.stockholmresilience.org/5.3d04209a18a2642b2fc162a3.htm, 2023. The irreversible and unpredictable effects of anthropogenic interventions that exceed planetary boundaries, as warned by Nordhaus, bring attention to scientific concerns about tipping points. These involve processes where sudden or irreversible changes occur as systems cross thresholds. Many of them operate at such a large scale that they are effectively unmanageable by humans with existing technologies. Four important global tipping points are the rapid melting of large ice sheets (such as Greenland), large-scale changes in ocean circulation such as the Gulf Stream, feedback processes where warming produces more warming, and enhanced warming over the long run. These tipping points are particularly dangerous because they are not easily reversed once they are triggered (NORDHAUS, W. *The Climate Casino: Risk, Uncertainty, and Economics for a Warming World*, p. 05. New Haven: Yale University Press, 2013).

Several political institutions are actively working on increasing "*decoupling*" to reevaluate economic growth and prosperity within the limits of our planet's resources. This change is illustrated by the European Union's adoption of circularity as its new economic paradigm.

In 2015, the EU launched the first EU Circular Economy Action Plan titled "*Closing the Loop*", which included measures to help stimulate Europe's transition towards a circular economy, boost global competitiveness, foster sustainable economic growth, and generate new jobs.

To further its objectives, the EU launched an updated plan in 2020 entitled "*Delivering a Circular Economy within the Planetary Boundaries*" as part of the European Green Deal[35]. This plan acknowledges the need to address and

---

[35] Introduced in 2019, the European Green Deal is a comprehensive set of policy initiatives with a long-term vision. Its primary objective is to achieve climate neutrality by 2050. However, it also has broader societal goals, such as promoting a fair and prosperous society with a modern and competitive economy. The Green Deal also promises to protect people from environmental harm and prioritize well-being and social inclusion in economic policy. Therefore, the Green Deal is considered a general policy framework rather than a specific law. It designs objectives and aspirations across various policy domains, which encompasses eight focus areas: 1) Increasing the EU's climate ambition for 2030 and 2050; 2) Providing clean, affordable, and secure energy; 3) Mobilizing industry for a clean and circular economy; 4) Building and renovating in an energy and resource-efficient way; 5) Aiming for zero pollution to create a toxic-free environment; 6) Preserving and restoring ecosystems and biodiversity; 7) Farm to Fork: promoting a fair, healthy, and environmentally friendly food system; and 8) Accelerating the transition to sustainable and smart mobility. The EU Green Deal underscores the significance of a holistic and cross-sectoral approach, where all relevant policy areas work together to advance its main goals: achieving a carbon-

reduce pressures on natural resources caused by consumption while aiming to create sustainable growth and jobs. It is also a prerequisite to achieve the EU's 2050 climate neutrality target and to halt biodiversity loss.

Amsterdam is the first city in the world to officially adopt the Doughnut economic development model as part of its strategy to achieve a fully circular city by 2050. The city is organizing a network of various political actors, including local authorities, communities, and companies, to work together towards common goals: to significantly reduce the use of new raw materials and promote well-being.

The ultimate goal of the city is to create a zero-impact urban environment that prioritizes circular strategies. These strategies aim to balance economic growth with protecting individuals and nature. Additionally, Amsterdam plans to become a *'Climate Neutral'* city by 2050, aspiring to mitigate its CO_2 emissions to 95% below 1990 levels. This will be achieved by focusing on buildings, transport, electricity, industry, and the port[36].

---

neutral European Union by 2050 and decoupling economic growth and resource use (EUROPEAN COUNCIL. *What is the European Green Deal?* Available at: https://www.consilium.europa.eu/en/policies/green-deal/#what).

[36] *Amsterdam Circular Strategy 2020-2025* and *The Amsterdam City Doughnut: A Tool for Transformative Action.* Available at: https://www.amsterdam.nl/en/policy/sustainability/circular-economy/, 2020.

As the Doughnut comprehends a device to implement these strategies, Raworth scaled the model to provide Amsterdam with a "*city portrait*" showing where basic needs are not being met and "planetary boundaries" overshot. One example can be recognized in the question "*What would it mean for the people of Amsterdam to thrive?*" regarding housing, which demonstrated the problem between sustaining basic needs and supporting excessively high rental costs.

The city target is the sufficient availability of affordable and decent homes, and the snapshot based on the Doughnut revealed that "*in 2018, almost 60,000 home seekers applied online for social housing, while only 12% were successful. Overall, almost 20% of city tenants cannot cover their basic needs after paying monthly rent*".

The first solution would be to build more, but this would have a negative impact on the environment due to the import of construction materials and their high greenhouse gas emissions. For this reason, the city encouraged builders to use recycled or bio-based materials as much as possible[37].

Amsterdam has set an ambitious target to reduce raw material consumption by 50% by the year 2030 and to

---

[37] BOFFEY, D. *The Guardian: Amsterdam to embrace 'doughnut' model to mend post-coronavirus economy*. Available at: https://www.theguardian.com/world/2020/apr/08/amsterdam-doughnut-model-mend-post-coronavirus-economy, 2020.

eliminate the average citizen's annual 41 kg of food waste by the same year. The city is actively collaborating with restaurants and hotels to implement measures aimed at minimizing food waste.

Additionally, Amsterdam has launched several initiatives to encourage the recycling of furniture, clothing, and electronics. These initiatives involve expanding the availability of "*libraries of things*", establishing second-hand markets and creating dedicated centers where people can learn how to repair various items.

Recently, the transformative potential of doughnut economics has been harnessed to redesign businesses, innovating their purposes, networks, governance, ownership, and finance. The aim is to make these businesses regenerative and distributive in their strategies, operations, and impacts, ultimately steering the global economic system towards a thriving future. The proposals outlined in the Doughnut Economics guide for businesses include adopting circular strategies such as innovating product design, eliminating single-use plastics and built-in obsolescence, as well as committing to paying living wages to the supply-chain workers who make the products[38].

---

[38] SAHAN, E. et all. *What Doughnuts Economics means for Business: Creating Enterprises that are Regenerative and Distributive by Design.* Doughnuts Economics Action Lab.

According to Raworth, the doughnut model raises a crucial question: What does it mean to grow? Are we sure that an increase in GDP should be the sole focus of our choices, or does development mean something else? This is especially true considering that our current economic model has led to an overshoot of planetary boundaries and fragile systems that have caused multiple financial crises[39].

Reflecting on this consideration, we must recognize that economic growth should enhance well-being; this should be our ultimate goal. As a result, we should phase out economic models that produce ill-being and focus on those who strive to achieve well-being. To get there, we need reliable and timely measures of human well-being based on a circular mindset.

---

[39] The increasing vulnerability of our social, economic, and political systems highlights the emergence of a complex scenario in which a multitude of present and future global risks interact with each other to form a *"polycrisis"* - a cluster of interconnected global risks with compounding effects, creating a challenging global landscape. For instance, resource rivalries represent a potential cluster of interconnected environmental, geopolitical, and socioeconomic risks associated with the supply and demand for natural resources. A problem becomes a crisis when it challenges our ability to handle it and thus threatens our identity. In a polycrisis, multiple disparate shocks occur, but their interactions intensify, making the overall situation even more overwhelming than the sum of the parts. At times, this can lead to a feeling of disconnection from reality (TOOZE, A. *Welcome to the World of the Polycrisis*, Financial Times n. 28, 2022).

2. SUSTAINABLE DEVELOPMENT AND CIRCULAR ECONOMY

2.1. Sustainable Development

Sustainable development is linked to how we manage and replenish our natural resources under a growth-based scenario to comprehensively improve the quality of life.

According to Pearce and Turner, sustainable development "*involves maximizing the net benefits of economic development, subject to maintaining the services and quality of natural resources over time*". Thus, it aims to balance the goals of economic prosperity and attend to environmental and social concerns harmoniously to enhance the intergenerational well-being[40].

Of course, the concept of sustainable development is not unanimous and has been subject to extensive debates during the last 40 years. However, the historical trajectory of the institutionalization of sustainable development can explain a lot about its definition, providing a solid ground to understand the elements present in its triple dimension encompassed by the ideas of economic growth, social equity, and environmental protection.

---

[40] WORLD BANK. *World Development Report 2003: Sustainable Development in a Dynamic World--Transforming Institutions, Growth, and Quality of Life.* Available at: http://hdl.handle.net/10986/5985, 2003.

First, we must analyze the roots of one of its components: the concept of development that remains hard to define in universally acceptable terms[41]. Historically, the concept of development was embedded in the evolution of the capitalist system and its expressions through industrialization and colonialism that intensified economic asymmetries between individuals, groups, and nations. Therefore, development was understood as an economic concept related to a process that results in economic growth and improves people's well-being[42].

During the 1960s, the idea of development was essentially focused on the quantitative performance of economic growth such as illustrated by the theory of Walt

---

[41] The lack of a universally accepted definition of development leads us to reflect on the values, principles, and norms that influence its different conceptions and frameworks. A starting point is the investigation of its semantical meaning in which the concept of development is linked to growth (or progress) and its different aspects, as together they create further growth (or progress). According to the Cambridge Dictionary, development is when someone or something grows or changes and becomes more advanced. From this definition, for instance, it is possible to relate the development concept with variation and innovation, among other ideas.

[42] During industrialization, capitalism was seen as a way to provide access to multiple benefits for most of society (DESAI, R. Theories of Development. In *Introduction to international development: Approaches, actors, issues, and practice*. Oxford University Press Canada pp. 44-46, 2017). By building different power relations based on dependency and on structural transformations in different aspects of life, colonialism forged our current perception of the "Global North" (the developed) and the "Global South" (the underdeveloped), contributing to understanding the concept of development (WILLIS, K. *Theories and practices of development. Routledge perspectives on development*. Routledge, pp. 20-21, 2011).

Rostow's Five Stages of Economic Growth, in which development is based on the progressive improvement of technological factors of production to achieve high mass consumption[43].

By the 70s, development specialists acknowledged that economic growth by itself would not be able to improve the conditions of well-being for global society without a more equitable consumption of natural resources to reduce its environmental impacts[44].

In this context, a new concept of development arose also centered on its qualitative aspects to consider the improvement of well-being and environmental protection, asserting an effortless awareness: if global economic growth affects the living ecosystems we depend on, compromising the welfare of present and future generations, it could not be sustained for too long[45].

---

[43] ROSTOV, W. W. *The Stages of Economic Growth: A Non-Communist Manifesto*. Cambridge University Press, 1991.

[44] In this period, we already had some disquiet about the adverse effects of production and consumption standards on health and the environment, warned by the UN Scientific Conference on the Conservation and Use of Resources in 1949 and by the Paris Biosphere Conference in 1968. In 1972, the Rome Club published the report "Limits of Growth" a pioneering document to awaken ecological consciousness about the use of natural resources and environmental degradation with a clear message that still holds today: "*Man can create a society in which he can live indefinitely on earth if he imposes limits on himself and his production of material goods to achieve a state of global equilibrium with population and production in carefully selected balance*" (MEADOWS, D. H. et al. *The Limits to Growth: A Report for the Club of Rome's Project on the Predicament of Mankind*. New York: Universe Books, 1972).

Hence, instead of emphasizing short-term gains, our economic system should point out long-term sustainable growth strategies to ensure a better quality of life for people, inserting "*sustainable development*" as a critical concept in development studies and political practices. According to this early idea of sustainable development, neglecting the environment can threaten global ecosystems and humanity[46].

In line with this idea, the report "*Our Common Future*" of the UN Brundtland Commission of 1987 introduced the classic definition of sustainable development: "*Sustainable development is the development that meets the needs of the present without compromising the ability of future generations to meet their own needs*".

Although the report has been marked by several criticisms, due to the absence of a program to implement actions to progress on sustainable development as well as the vagueness of its definition[47], the Brundtland report stressed the need for an integrated/holistic approach to understanding

---

[45] The conditions of time and space that influence the development process are relevant to understand the concept of sustainability as it refers to the arrangement of technological, scientific, environmental, and social systems in such a way that the resulting heterogeneous system can be maintained in a state of temporal and spatial equilibrium (NATH, B., HENS, L. and DEVUYST, D. *Sustainable Development*. VUB Press, 1996).

[46] CHESHIRE, D. *The Handbook to Building a Circular Economy*.RIBA publishing, 2021.

[47] BERCKERMAN, W. *Sustainable Development: Is It a Useful Concept?* Environmental. Values 3: 191-209, 1994.

the concept of Sustainability based on its economic, social, and environmental perspectives.

In 1992, the first UN Conference on Environment and Development (UNCED), also known as the Earth Summit, approved the 21 Agenda, which assigned to Nation-States the accountability for the adoption of a model of sustainable development through institutional mechanisms that would boost social and economic progress while respecting the environment.

According to this document, information, integration, and participation configure the critical building blocks to help countries progress on sustainable development. Therefore, it attributes to everyone the condition of the user and provider of the information concerning sustainable development. It also highlighted the need to do business by integrating new approaches considering environmental and social concerns. Moreover, the agenda inserted public participation in decision-making processes as an essential prerequisite for sustainable development[48].

Another vital contribution of Agenda 21 refers to its Chapter 4, entitled "Changing Consumption Patterns" which included in the discussions on the environmental crisis not only productive issues but also the need to address, through

---

[48] KINGSLEY, N. *History, Principles and Concepts of Sustainability*. White World Publication, 2014.

strategies and policies, consumption practices that aim to contribute to "*new concepts of wealth and prosperity which allow higher standards of living through changed lifestyles and are less dependent on the Earth's finite resources*"[49].

The Earth Summit was a milestone for the UN system, which started implementing a broad series of programs, institutions, and international agreements to promote sustainable development globally. This Summit also established two critical documents on sustainable development: the Convention on Biological Diversity and the United Nations Framework Convention on Climate Change (UNFCCC)[50].

In 2000, the Millennium Development Goals (MDGs) was launched as an innovative agenda on sustainability with a focus on addressing poverty in its multiple dimensions, from environmental issues and human development to

---

[49] JACKSON, T. *Sustainable Consumption* in ATKINSON, G., DIETZ, S., NEUMAYER, E., Handbook of Sustainable Development, Edward Elgar Publishing, 2007.

[50] During the same period, all the movements at the UN brought more awareness about the criteria to measure the prosperity of Nation-States. It became evident that this could only be supported partially by the GDP criteria, demonstrating the need to search for a more holistic approach linked to the broad idea of development. One such alternative, institutionalized by the United Nations Development Programme and rooted in Amartya Sen's ideas, is the Human Development Index. This index measures a nation's prosperity based on factors such as longevity, knowledge, and standard of living, providing a more nuanced perspective on development. It is also relevant to mention the GINI index, which measures the distribution of income or consumption across a population and indicates the levels of inequalities in a country.

gender and racial equalities, among other fundamental human rights, which aimed to commit the members of the UN in developing a better future to the world society.

[51]

The Millennium agenda comprehended a starting point to improve the conception of human development at a planetary level. It constituted an essential framework for global governance based on settled goals to stimulate cooperation and solidarity between multiple actors within a set period.

The MDGs used the monitoring concept of objectives, indicators, and timelines as an integral component of their strategy to engage organizations and nation-states on what needed to change and when.

---

[51] Available at: https://www.un.org/development/desacontent/sustainable-development-goals

To this end, the MDGs exemplified the spirit of the human rights-based approach to development – linking matters of human development with the need for universal equality. There was never a time in history when organizations and states were so focused on similar development concepts and initiatives[52].

The achievement of the Millennium Development Goals (MDGs) faced significant challenges. Rob Van Tulder highlights the governance issues that contributed to the shortcomings of the MDGs. He argues that the goals were not ambitious enough to catalyze the necessary global changes in sustainable development. Often viewed as "*goals without means*", they were relatively vague and lacked precise indicators for addressing specific issues within individual countries. Furthermore, the MDGs did not cover critical topics, such as environmental sustainability related to consumption and production patterns[53].

Several key events also undermined the success of the MDG agenda over a short period. These included terrorist attacks in leading Western nations, the emergence of developing countries in the international political arena, and

---

[52] BESADA, H., POLONENKO, L. M. and AGARWAL, M. *Did the Millennium Development Goals Work? Meeting Future Challenges with Past Lessons*. Policy Press, 2017.
[53] VAN TULDER, R. *Business & The Sustainable Development Goals: A Framework for Effective Corporate Involvement*. Rotterdam School of Management, Erasmus University, Rotterdam, 2018.

the economic crisis of 2008. Other pressing global factors, such as the environmental crisis exacerbated by climate change, increasing inequalities, and unsustainable consumption on a global scale, also played a role in this setback.

2.2. The Rise of the SDGs

From 2012 onwards, the UN intensified the promotion of a global dialogue with different actors and stakeholders to formulate new post-2015 development goals.

In September 2015, the 17 Sustainable Development Goals (SDGs) were launched by the document *"Transforming Our World: The 2030 Agenda for Sustainable Development"* which was to elaborate upon and broaden the scope of the MDGs, representing an adaptation of the global agenda on social and human development to the new planetary challenges.

Compared to the MDGs, the SDGs are marked by a more horizontal and inclusive building process that involved the entire United Nations system, the Member Nation-States, and various actors and stakeholders from the civil society, the private sector, academia, and public opinion, reaching in a comprehensive proposal of goals and targets to bring forward plans to transform the planet towards more sustainable development paths.

The idea behind the SDGs was to go further into political and sensitive issues present in the global agenda that the MDGs had not explicitly confronted.

The SDGs intend to expand the contents of the MDGs and not just rewrite them, penetrating topics concerning environmental dimensions and interconnecting them with different aspects of social life, such as reducing inequalities and responsible consumption, among others.

Through adopting the 2030 Agenda, Nation-States decided to take the bold and transformative steps urgently needed to shift the world onto a sustainable and resilient path. As we embark on this collective journey, we pledge that no one will be left behind[54].

Therefore, the SDGs comprehend 17 interconnected global goals elaborated to be a "*blueprint for achieving a better and more sustainable future for all*". These 17 people-centered goals are integrated, stressing that everything depends on everything and balancing sustainable development's environmental, economic, and social dimensions.

In other words, the SDGs represent the core of the holistic planetary agenda for economic growth, social

---

[54] UNITED NATIONS – Sustainable Development knowledge platform. *Transforming our world: the 2030 Agenda for Sustainable Development.* https://sustainabledevelopment.un.org/post2015/transformingourworld, 2015.

inclusion, and environmental protection, orientating all global, regional, national, and local development endeavors until 2030.

[55]

The SDGs are considered a universal program pursued and applied to all countries worldwide, not only poor countries. Achieving the goals requires efforts on all fronts: governments, businesses, civil society, and individuals everywhere all have an essential role to play.

Therefore, our society must rethink its current destructive growth and development strategies and engage multiple actors in a process that harmonizes economics and the environment into their decision-making[56].

---

[55] Available at: https://www.un.org/development/desacontent/sustainable-development-goals-2
[56] CHESHIRE, D. *The Handbook to Building a Circular Economy*. RIBA

Of course, nation-states have a vital role in integrating economic and environmental factors in the legal policy sectors of countries backed by the international community.

However, sustainability needs full cooperation, and the Nation-States alone cannot promote these necessary changes. This scenario requires the engagement of multiple actors: businesses, NGOs, communities, and individuals, all of whom have their part in promoting sustainability.

Furthermore, the goals and targets of the 2030 Agenda are focused on a multi-stakeholder bottom-up process that involves quantitative and qualitative indicators to measure their progress and the pursuit of a broader set of financial resources to operationalize them. They have a set of targets that are measured with indicators.

At this moment, there are 169 targets, each of them with between 01 and 03 indicators comprising 232 approved indicators to measure the progress in the achievement of the SDGs.

An exciting approach to the SDGs is the Wedding Cake Model developed by Carl Folke and his team at the Stockholm Resilience Center[57] which aims to propose a system of hierarchy among the goals based on a holistic view

---

Publishing, 2021.
[57] FOLKE, C., et al. *Social-ecological resilience and biosphere-based sustainability science*. Ecology and Society, 21(3):41, 2016.

of its social, economic, and environmental perspectives. It aims to demonstrate a broad spectrum of multiple goals that can be achieved concerning the biosphere, society, and economy.

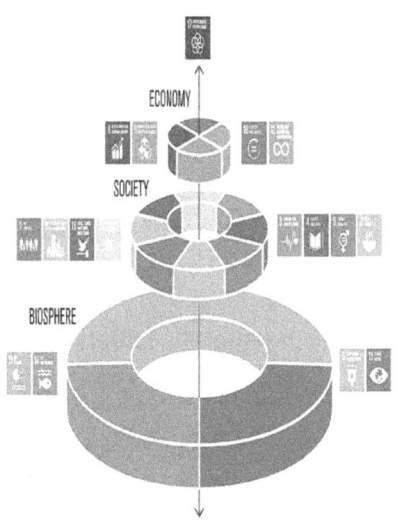

58

According to the Wedding Cake model, its layers provide a framework to establish the embedded interlinkages between different categories of SDGs.

The biosphere represents the "*foundation upon which prosperity and development ultimately rest*"; it means the basis of all SDGs upon which life exists and is sustained.

---

[58] Available at: https://www.stockholmresilience.org/research/research-news/2016-06-14-the-sdgs-wedding-cake.html.

Therefore, this model prioritizes the biosphere, which configures a precondition for economic growth and social well-being, establishing the limits of our planet to support human life.

The societies are characterized as man-made institutional conditions, and they contain the economies that symbolize the SDGs' organizational changing level.

At the top of the cake are the partnerships that comprehend the fundamental processes among multiple actors to promote transformational change toward sustainable development.

In 2021, after the global effects of the coronavirus pandemic (COVID-19), the United Nations published the Report "*Our Common Agenda*," which represents the Secretary-General's perspective on the future of international cooperation to better respond to humanity's most pressing challenges, primarily through the reinforcement of global solidarity and implementation of the SDGs.

This report symbolizes an inflection point for the idea of sustainable development as 2030 approaches, and we will need to rethink and update the SDGs and their mechanisms of governance[59].

---

[59] As it represents a historic shift for the UN regarding social and human development, the SDGs launched a novel type of governance based on goal-setting processes that present a set of peculiarities to deal with this new global agenda (BIERMANN, F., KANIEB, N. and KIM, R. *Global governance by goal-setting: the novel approach of the UN Sustainable*

2.3. The Sustainable Development Beyond SDGs

Of course, the institutional background provided by Agenda 2030 is essential to set common objectives and to coordinate efforts and policies to accelerate the implementation of existing agreements.

However, it is crucial to remember that sustainable development must go beyond the SDGs or any normative document. In addition to existing institutional agreements, the appearance of various environmental movements and NGOs in recent decades has also contributed to advances in sustainable development such as Green Peace, the World Wildlife Fund (WWF), the Environmental Defense Fund (EDF), and the Friends of the Earth[60].

At the current stage of our history, sustainability must be an integrated part of our lives to provide the means for our species to survive in harmony with the planet.

Ultimately, the evolution of sustainable development through the SDGs demonstrates a broader definition of

---

Development Goals. Current Opinion in Environmental Sustainability, 26: 26-31, 2017).

[60] According to Mertig, A. & Dunlap, R. (*Environmentalism: Preservation and Conservation. In N. J. Smelser, & P. B. Baltes, International Encyclopedia of the Social & Behavioral Sciences, pp. 4687-4693, Pergamon, 2001*), these movements influence international politics agenda to develop policies and disseminate environmental protection globally fostering initiatives to fight against pollution, loss of biodiversity, climate change and other threats that affect our ecosystems.

development, as it could encompass the entire process of transforming the economic and social backwardness of underdeveloped nations into a dynamic state of sustained economic growth and social well-being. However, its idea represents more than this process.

As a comprehensive societal process, sustainable development involves the interaction of multiple actors to cover all aspects of social life, providing an efficient method to combine the desire for environmental protection with the need for continued material and economic prosperity[61].

When it improves well-being within a legitimate institutional backdrop from political to legal frameworks surrounded by fairness and freedom, development enables people to pursue their existence with dignity.

As a transformative political program, it can be visualized as a strategy to design policies toward the objectives society aims to progress and comprehend the barriers and efforts that must be done effectively to implement them.

In this sense, sustainable development embraces all aspects of society and the engagement of its multiple actors (markets, governments, NGOs, cooperatives, and non-profit entities) to generate benefits not only for economic

---

[61] MOFFATT, I. *Sustainable Development: Principles, Analysis and Policies*. Parthenon: London, 1996.

prosperity but mainly for people's lives in a comprehensive manner that also include social equity and environmental protection to enhance holistically the intergenerational well-being.

As the SDGs demonstrate, the idea of sustainable development encompasses as ends in themselves higher incomes and much more: better education, higher standard of health and nutrition, less poverty, a cleaner environment, more equality of opportunity, greater individual freedom, and a more prosperous cultural life among other means to improve quality of life for present and future generations.

Global society must review its strategies of prosperity to progress in sustainable development, moving from the current linear process of economic growth to a holistic system that supports the triple dimension of sustainable development in different scales of governance.

In this context, the transition to a circular economy consists of a central vision to progress the number of SDGs to make the world healthier and more sustainable.

2.4. From Linear to Circular Economy

The idea of circularity is inspired by natural systems where there is no waste, meaning one species' waste becomes another species' food. If we replicate this idea in a manmade system, we could comprehend circularity as a systemic approach to economic development that is regenerative and distributive by design, aiming to progressively decouple economic growth from consuming our planet's limited resources.

The Circularity or Circular Economy follows the 3Rs approach: reduce, reuse, and recycle to integrate people and the planet as an essential part of the economic processes. According to the 3Rs approach to the circular economy, the resource consumption is minimized (reduced); the products or their components are repeatedly used without significant modification of their original purposes (reused); and, finally, the use of waste itself as resources transforming it into new products (recycled).

The linear economy system does not explore the full potential of products and their components. Once raw materials are collected, processed, and discarded after serving their intended purposes, they generate waste and pollution, adversely impacting our environment and compromising the quality of its services [62]. Conversely, the

---

[62] According to the World Bank Report "*Squaring the Circle: Policies from Europe's Circular Economy Transition*", the material management of the linear economic model—the extraction, production, transformation, transport, consumption, and disposal of materials used to make products and infrastructure—today accounts for 90 percent of total biodiversity loss and water stress impacts and 33 percent of health impacts due to air pollution. The production of goods and services in the linear economy occurs at the expense of ecosystems and the vital services they provide, causing the largest shares of responsibility for today's environmental burden (*"Squaring the Circle: Policies from Europe's*

circular economy aims to retain the value of products and components at a high rate by extending their lifetime period to the maximum.

Following the previous considerations, it is possible to highlight the insights provided by the European Commission about the concept of a circular economy where the value of products and materials is maintained for as long as possible, bringing significant economic benefits as it creates an optimal business environment for sustainable growth, job creation, and innovation[63].

Reflecting on the EU's definition, it is possible to perceive the relevance of value creation and how to transform it. These concepts are intrinsically attached to circularity. David Cheshire also emphasized this relationship when he mentioned that a shift to a more circular economy means not only using fewer resources but also creating and retaining value in building and their components that represent a positive legacy for future generations[64].

Circular Economy Transition" World Bank, 2022, p. 22. Available at: https://documents1.worldbank.org/curated/en/099425006222229520/pdf/P174596025fa8105a091c50fb22f0596fd1.pdf).

[63] EUROPEAN COMMISSION. Internal, Market, Industry, Entrepreneurship and SMEs, https://single-market-economy.ec.europa.eu/industry/sustainability_en#:text=Circular%20economy,Circular%20economy,again%20to%20create%20further%20value).

[64] CHESHIRE, D. *The Handbook to Building a Circular Economy*. RIBA Publisher, 2021. The author also underlined that the transition to circularity would create new business models and industries that would open space for long-term customer relationships and provide local employment opportunities from refurbishment and remanufacturing.

The transition from linear to circular economy represents a systemic transformation of how we create wealth through the production of goods and services and how we organize our society. It represents an opportunity to reconfigure our lifestyles, conciliating economic opportunities with environmental and social benefits.

This movement requires a meaningful social innovation process based on sustainable design decisions to rethink the logic of the values in which our global society operates and to identify where circular strategies come into play[65].

2.4.1. Circularity and Value Creation

The relation between value creation and circularity is relevant to understand what values are. According to Mariana Mazzucato, we can define value through multiple meanings, but in essence, it represents the production of new goods and services. How are these outputs produced (production), how are they shared across the economy

---

[65] There are different proposals to move our economic system towards circularity, such as the Cradle to Cradle, elaborated by William McDonough and Michael Braungart. According to their approach, the sustainable aspect of our economic system would be characterized by the creation of goods and services that generate ecological, social, and economic value; it means that we make money and not only avoid harming the environment and society but have a positive impact on both. (MCDONOUGH, W. and BRAUNGART, M. *Cradle To Cradle: Remaking The Way We Make Things,* San Francisco, CA: North Point Press, 2002).

(distribution), and what is done with the earnings that are created from their production (reinvestment)? Finally, it is also essential to comprehend the usefulness of what is being created: Are the products and services being created increasing or decreasing the resilience of the productive system?

Mazzucato continued her arguments by describing value creation as how different types of resources (human, physical, and intangible) are established and interact to produce new goods and services[66]. In this sense, value creation represents an interactive process that combines forces and different kinds of resources to turn them into something that meets the needs of others.

The previous considerations demonstrate how value creation represents the key driver of the economic process. It is traditionally considered a good or service that can be expressed financially, which means exchanged in the marketplace for money (or possibly other goods and services). Schenkel understood value creation as traditional supply chain objectives, customer satisfaction, and cost reduction, as well as environmental goals[67].

---

[66] MAZZUCATO, M. *The Value of Everything: Making and Taking in Global Economy*, p. 06. Penguin Books, 2019.
[67] SCHENKEL et al., *Understanding value creation in closed loop supply chains: Past findings and future directions. Journal of Manufacturing Systems*, 37(3), 729-745, https://doi.org/10.1016/j.jmsy.2015.04.009, 2015.

In this order of ideas, value creation can be analyzed through a business perspective as adding different elements to goods and services to intensify their purchase by customers, generating outputs that increase competitive advantage[68]. It is about transforming the value of something to provide a more excellent value.

In a linear economic system that prioritizes short-term gains, the logic of value creation is fundamentally based on financial performance. This monetization process of what is valuable has a clear consequence: the exclusion of what cannot be expressed financially with the externalization of costs and implicit values such as eco-services, including the decrease of biodiversity, density of insect populations, and a safe neighborhood[69].

---

[68] In business, competitive advantage refers to the elements that allow a company to outperform its rivals. It is related to a strategic position in the market that provides a company the capacity to produce goods and offer services better and cheaper than its competitors through the integration of different factors such as the approach to new technology and ability to innovate, access to natural resources, incorporation of highly skilled labor, geographic location, among others. One of the most prestigious studies on this topic was developed by Michael Porter and his Five Forces (Competitive Strategy: Techniques for Analyzing Industries and Competitors). He created a framework in which companies could understand the competitive scenario using five relevant criteria: a) how do new competitors enter the market? b) how are the dynamics of the existing competition? c) Can the customer replace the product/service with another at a similar price? d) Do customers have the power to lower the price? e) Do suppliers have the power to increase the price? This holistic approach allows companies to comprehend the competitive landscape better and select the proper strategy to acquire a competitive advantage.

[69] KOPNINA, H. and POLDNER, K. *Circular Economy: Challenges and*

From the circular economy perspective, the current logic of value creation must be reconsidered to cover broad purposes towards multiple dimensions simultaneously and not just financially.

Of course, innovative social strategies in line with the SDGs play a relevant role in this context as implementing this new logic affects a set of established paradigms such as production, consumption, and competition, among other essential drivers of the linear economic system.

The perspective based on multiple value creation aims to promote environmental protection, social inclusiveness, and financial purposes. In other words, the logic of value creation is not only centered on monetization but also on tackling social and environmental issues.

This paradigm shift can be visualized through the concept of the Triple Bottom Line conceived by Elkington (1998), which consists of an alternative accounting method based on sustainability that considers the commitment of business activities to three interconnected factors: profits, people, and planet[70].

Opportunities for Ethical and Sustainable Business. Routledge, 2021.

[70] The Social Bottom Line (People) aims to generate value for multiple stakeholders by positively impacting labor, social capital, and community, enhancing well-being. The Economic Bottom Line (Profit) connects a company's financial performance to the economy's development. Finally, the Environmental Bottom Line (Planet) is focused on minimizing the negative impact of the company's operation on nature and respecting the appropriate consumption of resources for present and

In other words, the success of a company is not just based on one bottom line, profits, and shareholder value; there are also environmental and social impacts as part of that equation[71].

Capturing the idea of the Triple Bottom Line in the circular economy, the logic of value creation is oriented to keep products, materials, and resources circulating at the value chain to their highest rate for as long as possible by reinserting them after they serve to their original purposes,

---

future generations. Elkington understood that the interaction of these three factors is the best path to progress on sustainability.

[71] Gimenez, C. Sierra, V. & Rodon, J. (Sustainable Operations: Their Impact on the Triple Bottom Line, International Journal of Production Economics, vol. 140, issue 1, 149-159, 2012) stated that, according to the Triple Bottom Line theory, companies have to act on three different bottom lines (economic, environmental, and social) to accomplish good results on their performance by achieving positive financial impact and incorporating environmentally and socially responsible behaviors.

reducing the extraction of raw material and the generation of waste, and ensuring quality of life and social inclusion[72].

In an influential article in the Harvard Business Review titled "*Creating Shared Value: How to Reinvent Capitalism—and Unleash a Wave of Innovation and Growth,*"[73] Michael Porter and Mark Kramer introduced the concept of shared value, which aims to ensure a company's competitiveness while contributing to the economic, social, and environmental well-being of the communities in which the company operates.

Porter and Kramer's vision proposes that companies can create shared value by reconceiving products and markets, redefining productivity in the value chain, and enabling local cluster development. This transformative power can lead to a more sustainable and prosperous future for all stakeholders.

One way to promote sustainability is by rethinking products and markets. This involves redesigning products to better meet societal and environmental needs and finding new market opportunities that align with these values. To

---

[72] The circular economy's business models improve how various stakeholders interact. This also increases accountability for where raw materials come from and the life cycles of products, contributing to the generation of closed-loop value chains.

[73] PORTER, M. and KRAMER, M. R. *Creating Shared Value: How to Reinvent Capitalism—and Unleash a Wave of Innovation and Growth. Harvard Business Review, January-February, 2011.*

achieve this, innovative methods such as sustainable design, circular economy principles, and stakeholder engagement are used. These methods aim to eliminate negative impacts and enhance positive ones for all stakeholders, thus contributing to the creation of shared value.

The productivity of the supply chain is connected to the opportunities and cost savings generated by shared value. This connection is evident in the various societal and environmental issues that impact and are affected by supply chains, including natural resource usage, water consumption, health and safety, working conditions, and fair treatment in the workplace.

Improving local clusters, including infrastructure and educational and skill development programs, presents an opportunity to unlock the potential of economies in which companies operate. This can result in improved productivity, innovation, and competitiveness.

The integration of shared value strategies into business practices is part of a virtuous circle. It requires a long-term perspective, but most importantly, it demands strong management leadership and unwavering commitment. Overcoming the challenges, including the need for investments and potential changes in corporate culture, is crucial to engaging different stakeholders in implementing shared value strategies.

Porter and Kramer concluded their article by emphasizing the importance of shared value in unlocking a more advanced form of capitalism. They proposed that this form of capitalism would reestablish the connection between company success and community success and would lead to a broader understanding of value creation. They pointed out that *"not all profits are equal, highlighting the idea that has been overlooked in the narrow, short-term focus of financial markets and in much management thinking. Profits with a social purpose represent a higher form of capitalism - one that will enable society to progress more rapidly while allowing companies to grow even further. This, in turn, leads to a positive cycle of company and community progress, ultimately resulting in enduring profits"*[74].

---

[74] One example of a company that successfully incorporates shared value strategies into the core principle of its business model is Tony's Chocolonely, a Dutch chocolate factory with a clear mission: to produce 100% slavery-free chocolate. Big chocolate companies often pay farmers who produce cocoa an inhumanely low price, even with the added certification premiums. This poverty directly contributes to issues like child labor and modern slavery. To combat structural poverty and promote fair relationships with cocoa cooperatives in Ghana and Côte d'Ivoire, Tony's Chocolonely established *"Tony's Open Chain"*, which includes five Principles of Collaboration for Slave-Free Cocoa: 1. *Traceable Beans*: The cocoa beans used for cocoa butter and cocoa mass in their bars are 100% traceable. 2. *A Higher Price*: They aim to bridge the gap between a living income and what a farmer currently receives for their beans. 3. *Strong Farmers' Cooperatives*: These cooperatives provide advantages such as helping farmers find international markets, organizing transport, offering training, and facilitating joint purchasing of agricultural resources. 4. *Long-Term Partnerships*: The company has signed five-year cooperation agreements with all cooperatives to guarantee sales for farmers, allowing them room for investment. 5. *Better*

The triple bottom line and shared value are innovative concepts that break away from conventional wisdom and offer multiple perspectives on value creation. They redefine value creation, considering societal and environmental issues as core matters that are equally important as profits. This redefinition guides businesses towards a more distributive and regenerative model aligned with circularity[75].

2.4.2. Circularity and the SDGs

Of course, the complexity of the strategies and collective actions involved in the transition towards circularity is incompatible with a one-size-fits-all solution rather than developing new ideas and approaches being designed and tested to promote the intended change towards circularity.

In this context, transforming the take-make-dispose system through a circular mindset provides a unique

---

Cocoa Quality: Improved productivity of at least 800 kg per hectare per year is required, which must be achieved without employing child labor. By following these principles, Tony's Chocolonely aims to positively impact the cocoa industry and integrate equity into its business strategies (TONY'S CHOCOLONELY. *Tony's Open Chain*. Available at: https://www.tonysopenchain.com/our-approach/tonys-5-sourcing-principles).

[75] When adapting business models to the value creation proposed by the circular model, it is essential to consider social and environmental factors in its structure, with a focus on specific strategies such as prolonging the use of materials, promoting durability, and using eco-design to simplify recycling and upcycling processes.

framework for progress on the 2030 Agenda. This path encompasses a holistic approach that cuts across various sectors representing our current global challenges, such as food and agriculture, energy, climate change, water, and sanitation.

Thus, circularity is considered a toolbox to progress on many SDG goals and targets. In any case, it is possible to identify a direct relation with SDG 12 as this goal aims to "*ensure sustainable consumption and production patterns*".

In this sense, circular economy closes the gap between the production/consumption and the natural cycles of our ecosystems to allow them to replenish and provide the essential elements to attend to human needs, reducing the pressure on the natural environment by improving resource efficiency the life cycle of existing material and products by re-using, repairing, refurbishing, and recycling[76].

The targets and indicators of SDG 12 also reveal the idea of circularity as they propose the sustainable management and efficient use of natural resources, the

---

[76] Benton, Hazell, and Hill stated that a circular economy approach stimulates companies to analyze their operations and their supply chains and reflect on how resources are sourced, how they can be used more efficiently, where they can be more effectively recovered, and where the need for raw materials can be designed out of the business model altogether. Together, these strategies add up to a greater understanding and control of the supply chain, reducing exposure to resource risks, avoiding reputational threats, and eliminating waste (BENTON, D., HAZELL, J. and HILL, J. *The Guide to the Circular Economy: Capturing Value and Managing Material Risk*, Routledge, 2017).

reduction of waste, the need to provide information and awareness for lifestyles in harmony with nature, the improvement of our scientific and technological capacity to move towards more sustainable patterns of consumption and production, among others.

For instance, in what concerns the scientific and technological aspects of the circular economy, which is directly aligned with SDG 9, innovation plays an essential role as its multiple perspectives can unlock the capacity and value of all kinds of assets through the 3Rs approach.

The option for a green recovery investing in sustainable growth will depend on how human society will deal with the long-term emerging risks from the historical environmental impact of the linear economic paradigm.

Therefore, the world response to the linear processes must be focused on addressing underlying factors through the SDGs based on circular strategies to recover prosperity and restructure our society in a healthier, safer, fairer, and more resilient path.

3. CIRCULAR ECONOMY: PRINCIPLES AND STRATEGIES

3.1. Principles of Circular Economy

The Circular Mindset is a new way of thinking about the economy to create a more sustainable and equitable future for all by complementing our notion of value to include environmental protection, conservation of natural resources, and social inclusion. It goes beyond the extractive model pledged by the linear "take-make-dispose" to decouple economic activity from consuming our planet's finite resources and focus on positive benefits to the environment and society.

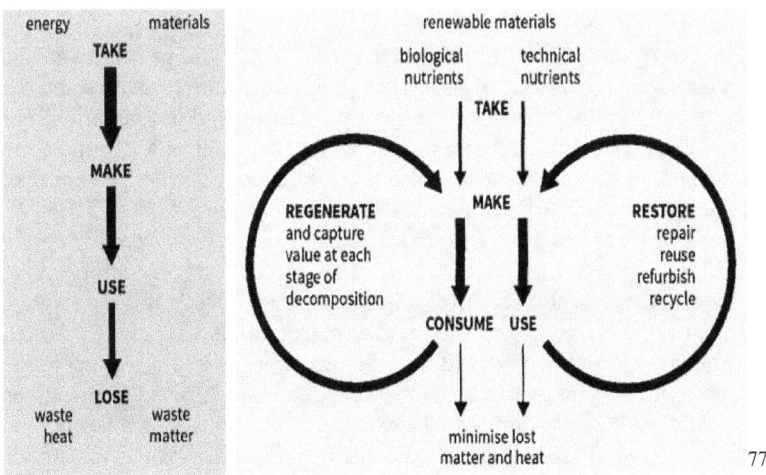

[77]

---

[77] DOUGHNUT ECONOMICS. *The Butterfly Diagram*. Available at: https://doughnuteconomics.org/about-doughnut-economics.

Understanding Circular Economy as a restorative and distributive model in which the natural and social systems coexist harmoniously to redefine growth and prosperity[78], it is relevant to reflect on its founding and interconnected principles: efficiency, sufficiency, and fairness. These principles represent the guiding ideas behind our strategies to transit toward circularity[79].

The efficiency comprehends the idea of doing more and better with less, reducing environmental impact through optimizing materials and energy. Efficient processes can manage the available resources to produce optimal results within particular technological possibilities.

---

[78] According to a study by Kirchherr et al. (2023), the principles of the circular economy are rooted in the recognition of finite resources and the need to rethink the linear paradigms of production and consumption. For instance, the concept of 'cradle to cradle', where products are designed to be reused or recycled, is a practical application of the principle of efficiency that aims to maximizing the value of resources (KIRCHHERR, J., YANG, N. N., SCHULZE-SPÜNTRUP, F. et al. *Conceptualizing the Circular Economy (Revisited): An Analysis of 221 Definitions*. In: Resources Conservation and Recycling, Vol. 194, 107001, 2023).

[79] Focusing on the regeneration and preservation of natural capital, Velenturf and Purnell affirmed that the principles of a circular economy promote growth, innovation, and resilience, with significant implications for sustainable development. They provide a holistic framework to address pressing global challenges such as resource scarcity, climate change, and waste management. For example, by promoting the regeneration and preservation of natural capital, the Circular Economy principles can help mitigate climate change by reducing greenhouse gas emissions and promoting sustainable resource use (VELENTURF, A. P., and PURNELL, P. *Principles for a sustainable circular economy*. Sustainable Production and Consumption, 27, p. 1437-1457, 2021).

Resource decoupling (or dematerialization) is an example of applying the principle of efficiency as it aims to reduce the use of materials, energy, water, and land resources for the same economic output. A straightforward way to demonstrate this process is by comparing the rise of economic output over time with the rise of resource input. When the last one is smaller, resource decoupling is happening.

Following the idea of achieving a more efficient and responsible use of natural resources, eco-innovation is also directly related to the principle of efficiency. According to Kemp and Person, eco-innovation is defined as *"the production, assimilation or exploitation of a product, production process, service or management or business method that is novel to the organisation (developing or adopting it) and which results, throughout its life cycle, in a reduction of environmental risk, pollution and other negative impacts of resources use (including energy use) compared to relevant alternatives"*[80].

The Ecodesign for Sustainable Products Regulation (ESPR), a significant initiative that came into effect in July 2024, clearly demonstrates the European Union's commitment to making environmentally sustainable products

---

[80] KEMP, R. and PERSON, P. *Measuring Eco-Innovation: Consumption*, OECD. Available at: https://www.oecd.org/env/consumption-innovation/43960830.pdf, 2008.

the norm in Europe and enhancing its resource independence through efficiency.

The ESPR is a complete framework aimed at reducing the environmental impacts of products throughout their entire lifecycle. It achieves this by advocating for the efficient use of resources through comprehensive sustainability standards. This approach not only reduces greenhouse gas emissions and minimizes waste but also demonstrates the EU's dedication to achieving climate neutrality by 2050.

The directive addresses various aspects of a product's lifecycle, including carbon footprint, resource efficiency, durability, repairability, and recyclability. Its aim is to promote eco-design, prolong product lifespan, and reduce waste.

An innovative aspect of the ESPR is the introduction of the Digital Product Passport (DPP), which provides detailed information about a product's environmental impact, the materials used in its manufacture, and recommendations for recycling or disposal. This tool enhances transparency and access to information, empowering consumers and stakeholders to make informed decisions.

At the private sector, an interesting example of a business strategy toward efficiency is Dell Computer Corporation, which represents a company committed to reducing – and eventually eliminating – environmentally sensitive substances and keeping material out of landfills.

To this end, one of the company's goals is to design its products by using less and more environmentally friendly materials, optimizing reusability, repairability, and recyclability, and ensuring integrated energy efficiency from renewable sources. The company has developed guidelines for its recycling partner to ensure *"that hardware is demanufactured, that no environmentally sensitive waste is exported to third-world countries and that suppliers' processes maximize the number of materials recovered for reuse"*.

Concerns about long service life, easy upgrades, and problem-free repairs are part of Dell's strategies to avoid waste. For example, over 90% of a typical Dell laptop is recyclable. Moreover, the company sells around 800.000 returned and remanufactured products annually in its Global Dell Outlet[81].

Another important circular strategy Dell implemented is transitioning from the physical elements of value creation towards virtualization, optimizing resources used in its operations. Aiming to perform its activities paperless, the

---

[81] DELL TECHNOLOGIES. *Accelerating the Circular Economy to Reduce Waste and Protect the Planet.* Available at: https://www.dell.com/en-us/dt/corporate/social-impact/advancing-sustainability/accelerating-the-circular-economy.htm#anchor.

whole process for purchasing Dell's computer is online, as well as customer support.

According to their report, Dell states its circular purposes, from product concept and development to end-of-product-life practices and offerings. It follows strict environmental standards beyond compliance to meet its customers' expectations for responding to societal and environmental needs[82].

Therefore, efficiency is about the absence of waste and allocation of resources to attend to people's needs at the least possible cost, respecting the ultimate ratio to utilize specific means in the circular economy: achievement of well-being. In this perspective, if one system produces goods and services that nobody consumes and affects the quality of life, it is inefficient.

Sufficiency is the second principle that complements the circular economy mindset, characterized by the adequate consumption of goods and services necessary for our well-being. It is represented by the idea of a middle path, promoting a balanced and beneficial prosperity for people and the planet.

Through sufficiency, it is possible to prevent underconsumption, monitor overconsumption, and

---

[82] DELL. *Environmental Report: Sustainability*. Available at: https://i.dell.com/sites/doccontent/corporate/creating/model/sustainability/environment/cr-report-2003.

effectively address poverty. This reassures the balance it can bring to our consumption patterns and its potential to protect our natural systems.

Sufficiency must be comprehended as a path of living/behaving for people and institutions of all social levels that are developed step-by-step, starting from creating financial self-immunity. After the sensible progress of the economic foundations, it is possible to advance on the following steps to seek to increase revenues.

According to the Thai development model, the "*Sufficiency Economy Philosophy*" (SEP) can be a valuable way to illustrate the principle as one of the foundations of the circular economy.

Sufficiency thinking is designed to help people live within their means and to be resilient to shocks and stresses. It is based on three interdependent and interconnected pillars that are useful for analyzing situations, identifying objectives, setting plans, and making decisions at any level of society:

1) *Moderation* means sufficiency at a level of not doing something too little or too much at the expense of oneself or others, for example, producing and consuming at a moderate level and according to one's mean - not maximizing short-term profitability but balancing it with long-term sustainability.

2) *Reasonableness* refers to rational decisions and consideration of the factors involved and careful anticipation of the outcomes that may be expected from them, considering their multiple impacts - sufficiency thinking requires extensiveness and thoughtfulness in planning, carefulness in applying knowledge, and implementing those plans.

3) *Prudence* involves assessing and managing risks in future scenarios and achieving a level of competence and self-reliance before proceeding to the next steps of a venture. When companies are "*perseverant*" and "*resilient*", they can keep up with expected and unexpected changes as they continuously develop themselves in many essential aspects.

Decisions and activities must be carried out at a sufficient level depending on two conditions: knowledge, comprising all-around knowledge in the relevant fields, and morality (or virtues), which refers to integrity, ethical behavior, hard work, honesty, and perseverance.

For the moral/ethical conditions, Sufficiency Thinking enforces the conditions that people are to possess – honesty and integrity – while conducting their lives with perseverance, harmlessness, and generosity[83].

---

[83] CONTIPELLI, E and PICCIAU, S. *Post-COVID-19: Rebuilding Our Paradigms Through Sustainable Development Goals and the Sufficiency Economy Philosophy*. New York: IndraStra Global, 2020.

Applying the three pillars (moderation, reasonableness, and prudence) together with the two conditions of knowledge and morality leads to progress in acquiring sustainable and resilient balance in the four dimensions of life: economic, environmental, social, and cultural.

The SEP plays a crucial role in enhancing overall human well-being. It focuses on alleviating poverty by reducing people's vulnerabilities, strengthening their capabilities, and shaping their lives. These efforts show the strong connection between SEP and SDGs as they share common objectives.

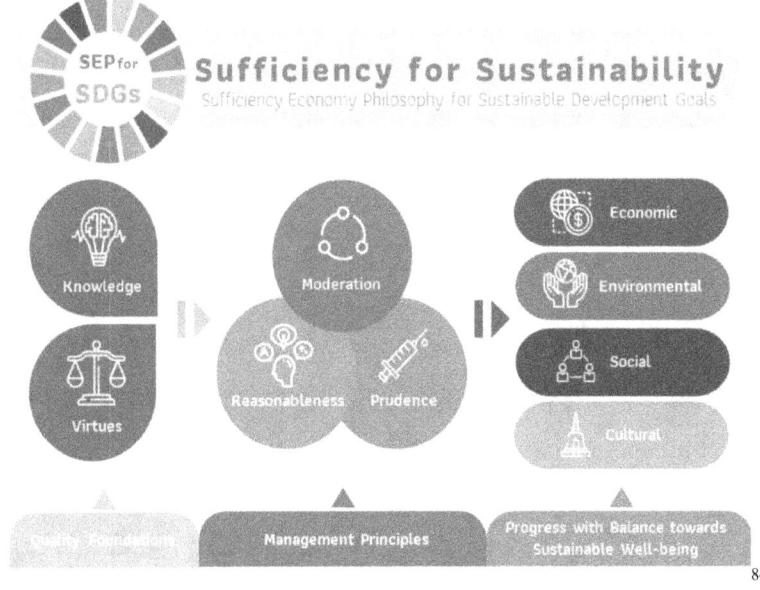

The Thailand Sustainable Development Foundation scheme illustrates the connection between the SEP and the SDGs. By focusing on the quality conditions of knowledge and virtues (morality) and applying the three management principles, it is possible to achieve sustainable well-being in four aspects of life: economic, environmental, societal, and cultural. Each of the 17 SDGs is related to one of these four aspects.

With its wide application, the SEP benefits individuals and private businesses at local and national levels and serves as a powerful approach to contributing to progressing on the SDGs at the global level.

In business, the Bathroom Design Company Limited presents itself as a case related to applying sufficiency thinking. The company provides a full range of innovative bathroom-related products such as bathtubs, ceramic sanitary ware, shower enclosures, massage and shower panels, utility shelves, and other bathroom accessories. Its growth strategy is based on moderation, as the company avoids overly ambitious goal commitments, avoids overextending its loans, and values long-term partnerships over short-term profits.

---

[84] THAILAND SUSTAINABLE DEVELOPMENT FOUNDATION. *Sufficiency for Sustainability*. Available at: http://tsdf.nida.ac.th/en/, 2018.

Emphasizing that moderation and growth are not mutually exclusive, nor is moderation at odds with good business opportunities, Orose Leelakulthanit explained that Bathroom Design Company has remained in its area of expertise, respecting its core competency, carefully using its available resources, and looking at profitability and the relationship of debt with equity and time interest expenses. He continues to analyze the company, highlighting that the growth of Bathroom Design has been quite extraordinary, and they have produced at least seven lines of bathtubs for almost 30 countries in the world—all within a decade of operations[85].

The Sufficiency Economy Philosophy promotes careful consideration of the business impact on all stakeholders, especially the community and the environment. It focuses on long-term strategies through the application of its principles and conditions to tackle unethical business practices. Most importantly, it also stands firmly on the

---

[85] LEELAKULTHANIT, O. *The Factors Affecting Life in Moderation*. Asian Social Science; Vol. 13, No. 1; 2017. Available at: http://dx.doi.org/10.5539/ass.v13n1p106. Furthermore, Bathroom Design invests in innovation to add value and benefits to all its stakeholders through green technologies, such as recycling the water used to test its bathtubs during the quality control stage. Acrylic materials, leftover from sanitary ware manufacturing, are transformed into cabinets, bookshelves, shoe racks, and even buttons for staff to wear in the company trade shows.

belief that profitability and social responsibility are not always in opposition to one another.

Finally, equity appears as the principle of the circular economy directly focused on its social aspects to provide impartial and just treatment to people according to their needs without favoritism or discrimination.

However, as with any normative concept, it is essential to remember that the concept of equity does not have a precise definition that can be applied rigorously. Historically, *"equity"* has had different interpretations; it means different things to different people. For thousands of years, philosophers have wrestled with the principles of justice based on equity and fairness that should guide social decisions. They will probably wrestle with such questions for thousands of years to come[86]. Among its variable meanings and views, a common denominator on equity relates it to fairness, whether locally in families and communities or globally across nations[87].

Thus, equity includes the idea of fairness to guide the redistribution of income and wealth in a way that is right or reasonable to alleviate poverty and reduce inequality. Poverty involves the lack of income and the resources to

---

[86] CASE, Karl E. and FAIR, Ray C. *Principle of Economics*, p. 13. New Jersey: Pearson Prentice Hall, 2004.
[87] WORLD DEVELOPMENT REPORT. *Equity and Development, p. 18*. New York: A copublication of The World Bank and Oxford University Press, 2006.

guarantee livelihoods, such as hunger and malnutrition, limited access to education, and other essential personal and social development capabilities.

Inequality encompasses the unjust distribution of resources and opportunities among members of a given society, and equity can help tackle it by eliminating discriminatory laws, policies, and practices to enhance equal opportunities for poorer groups.

The principle of equity is mainly expressed through the distributive aspect of the circular economy. This approach addresses wealth concentration, inequality, and marginalization through long-term partnerships between multiple stakeholders and developmental strategies. It aligns with the different interests of policymakers, economists, environmentalists, and individuals concerned with social justice.

Consider the substantial growth in jobs associated with the circular economy in the EU. Between 2012 and 2018, this sector experienced a 5% increase, reaching approximately 4 million jobs[88]. Acquiring skills necessary for a green transition is expected to boost job creation further, effectively linking the circular and social economy[89].

---

[88] EUROSTAT. *Circular Economy: Job Creation*. Available at: https://ec.europa.eu/eurostat/tgm/refreshTableAction.do?tab=table&plugin=1&pcode=cei_cie010&language=en.

[89] The European Pillar of Social Rights and the Pact for Skills aim to enhance investments in education and training systems, lifelong learning,

In this context, the concept of "*just transition*" emerges as a tool for fairness to guarantee that the significant advantages of transitioning to a circular economy are distributed equitably. It also aims to support those who may suffer economically as a result of this transition, including countries, regions, industries, communities, workers, or consumers[90].

As part of the EU's Green Deal, the Just Transition Mechanism aims to ensure a fair transition to a climate-neutral economy, mitigating the social and economic impacts. It focuses on assisting regions, industries, and workers that will encounter the most significant challenges. The mechanism aims to mobilize at least €100 billion through various funding schemes, providing financial support, guiding investments with transition plans for regions, offering attractive conditions and risk-sharing for both private and public investors, and providing technical assistance.

---

and social innovation to accelerate the transition towards circularity while supporting capacity building and job creation. The strategies mentioned in the documents illustrate the distributive perspective of this transition based on equity.

[90] The concept of just transition is not just a local or regional concern, but a global one, widely recognized in different international agreements such as the Paris Agreement. This agreement acknowledges 'the imperatives of a just transition of the workforce and the creation of decent work and quality jobs in accordance with nationally defined development priorities.' This global recognition underscores the importance of employment in addressing climate change, making it a united effort.

In the developing world, countries are also taking action to establish public policies that accelerate the transition to a circular economy. For instance, in June 2024, Brazil launched its first National Circular Economy Strategy (ENEC). This strategy is based on resource efficiency and the productive regeneration of nature. It also emphasizes the active involvement of workers in the circular economy to foster lasting and more conscious economic growth.

The Brazilian strategy showcases the country's dedication to building an inclusive circular economy that embodies the principle of equity. It focuses on the idea of a fair transition and recognizes the significance of policies that ensure the active participation of workers in remanufacturing, reuse, maintenance, and recycling markets. It also considers the impact on agricultural workers and natural ecosystems, ensuring that their health is not compromised during the transition.

Several companies are adopting distributive strategies by establishing long-term commitments along their value chain through fair trade practices with producers, workers, and stakeholders affected by their operations to integrate equity components into their operations.

One example of the application of the principle of equity is the French sustainable footwear company VEJA. The company operates based on the ideas of fair trade and ecological materials. The organic cotton used in its production is sourced from certified farmer associations in Brazil and Peru, who do not use chemicals to create their materials. These relationships are based on long-term partnerships in a fair trade agreement.

Furthermore, VEJA also attempted to improve the working conditions of the whole production chain, ensuring they were met without any exceptions. For example, such notions are considered: housing conditions, how groups are treated, and if they could defend their rights on any matter if the standards developed by VEJA are met if all employees are granted benefits and freedom of expression[91].

The core of the concept of equity in the context of sustainable development includes a strong dedication to fairness, particularly for future generations. As suggested by Robert O'Brien and Marc Williams, sustainable development policies should steadfastly aim to guarantee that the well-being of future generations is not inferior to our own.[92]

Equity involves applying a global perspective to ensure the well-being of all communities, providing equal access to resources, health, privileges, and opportunities,

---

[91] VEJA. Production/VEJA. Available at: https://project.veja-store.com/en/single/production, 2021.
[92] O'BRIEN, R. and WILLIAMS, M. *Global Political Economy: Evolution and Dynamics*, p. 308. New York: Palgrave MacMilliam, 2004.

while acknowledging historical disparities within and across nations and people.

3.2. Circular Strategies

Following the guidelines provided by the principles of efficiency, sufficiency, and equity, the circular strategies are based on the following actions: eliminating waste, keeping products and materials in use, and regenerating natural systems.

The circular economy is inspired by the natural systems in which waste does not exist. One species' waste becomes another species' food. According to the idea of "*Waste is Food*", we shift from a notion of waste – a material with no or little value, to a notion of a by-product, no longer directly useful to its last user but potentially a valuable resource for other actors in the system[93].

More specifically, in the circular economy, waste builds capital, and today's goods become tomorrow's resources.

Hence, waste management configures one of the main pillars of the concept of circular economy, as stated by Preston: "*A circular economy is an approach that would transform the function of resources in the economy. Waste*

---

[93] MCDONOUGH, W. and BRAUNGART, M. *Cradle To Cradle: Remaking The Way We Make Things,* San Francisco, CA: North Point Press, 2002.

from factories would become a valuable input to another process–and products could be repaired, reused or upgraded instead of thrown away"[94].

The circular framework encompasses implementing strategies that emphasize optimizing resource use and mitigating waste production, encouraging innovative methods throughout the value chain to design out waste from the beginning rather than focusing only on waste recycling at the end of the chain.

Circularity aims to keep products and services in use and retain their value at a high rate in so-called "loops." It means that if the products and services can provide value while simultaneously promoting activities that reduce the need for the material per unit of value produced, they will be part of the supply chain over and over again instead of being disposed of at landfills. These activities involve, for example, service-based offerings such as rental services, the creation of more durable and leaner products, and increasing the use of recycled materials[95].

A closed-loop supply chain utilizes the traditional supply chain (forward logistics) with reverse logistics, considering the product after being used for its original

---

[94] PRESTON, F. *A Global Redesign? Shaping the Circular Economy.* Chantam House: Briefing Paper, 2012.
[95] ZHU et al. *Confirmation of a Measurement Model for Green Supply Chain Management Practices Implementation*, International Journal of Production Economics 111(2), 2010.

purposes. Once the product is manufactured, shipped, and distributed through a reseller, the manufacturer works to encourage the return of the product when it is no longer functional or needed. Reverse logistics kick in, and products can be repaired, resold, or split for reuse in future products.

This strategy maximizes the idea of value-generating as many "*loops*" as possible to reduce the extraction of natural resources and the production of waste. In other words, "waste" or other system outputs (secondary raw materials, valuables) are reincluded in the value chain, enabling several additional cycles at a high rate. Systemically, the order is recovered and reused as many components and parts of the products and services as possible.

The regenerative aspect of the circular economy involves two types of material flows: biological nutrients are designed to re-enter the biosphere safely (through composting or other approaches), and technical nutrients (non-biological materials) are designed to be used again with minimal energy and highest quality retention Considering this idea, regenerative strategies use innovation to promote a radical change in how materials circulate throughout the economy more sustainably.

For example, plastics would be originated from plants instead of fossil fuels. Nanotechnology and Biotechnology could improve the quality of products, increasing their durability and other beneficial properties. At the end of the life cycle, the product would biodegrade or could be detached to be reinserted in the value chain.

In addition, regeneration is attached to the factor of time to provide our natural system the capacity to replenish itself and meet society's needs sustainably.

Thus, the transition to circularity involves a shifting behaviour through technological, organizational, and social innovative processes. The economic system must be regenerative by designing eco-friendly materials, having a low carbon footprint, avoiding planned obsolescence, and using other methods that respect our planet and people.

3.2.1. Circularity and SDG Targets

The circularity comprises the expression of a paradigm shift that requires profound changes in the living standards of the global society. As this path aims to integrate nature as an inspiration to our productive and consumption systems to respond to social and environmental needs, the transition towards circularity aims to address the so-called wicked problems or *"complex, intractable, open-ended"*[96] problems that need multiple solutions instead of one.

---

[96] HEAD, B. W. and ALFORD, J. *Wicked Problems: Implications for Public Policy and Management*, p. 101. *Administration and Society.*

Wicked problems do not have one-size-fits-all solutions, requiring holistic approaches to establishing which strategies to adopt[97] that should carve out solutions for the whole dimension of the problem, incorporating the interrelations between all the causal factors and policy objectives.

In this attempt to cover the whole wickedness of issues, these holistic strategies must involve the positive engagement of all stakeholders (businesses, governments, communities, and individuals); they all have an essential role in demonstrating their interconnections and the broader picture of the problem.

By using the targets of the SDG 12 associated with individual goals, it is possible to shape convergent strategies throughout different public and private institutions, generating synergies to overcome wickedness and impacting the system transformations to transit towards circularity.

47(6) 711-739, 2015.

[97] RITTEL, H. W. J. and WEBBER, M. M. *Dilemmas in a General Theory of Planning*. *Political Sciences*. 4, 155-169, 1973. Rittel and Weber elaborated a set of characteristics to define and explain the challenges related to wicked problems. The wicked problems do not have one single definition as they will always be contested by multiple stakeholders. They are interconnected, generating mutual symptoms in each other. They do not present a "stopping rule", it means a definitive solution. Their solutions can be positive or negative according to the stakeholders involved and are configured as a *"one-shot operation"* and the experimentation of their social effects cannot be made undone. There is an exhaustive list of potential solutions for all wicked problems.

Considering this scenario, SDG 12 and its targets offer a roadmap to ensure responsible production and consumption systems by closing the loop between resource and waste, strengthening the respect for the limits of our planet on which the future development (or survival) of humanity depends.

The concept of Sustainable Consumption and Production can be defined as *"the use of services and related products, which respond to basic needs and bring a better quality of life while minimizing the use of natural resources and toxic materials as well as the emissions of waste and pollutants over the life cycle of the service or product so as not to jeopardize the needs of future generations"*[98]

The previous definition reveals a set of elements that are covered by the idea of circularity:

• The use of products and services that refer to "*basic needs*" expresses the sufficiency principle.

• To promote "*a better quality of life*" as the goal proposed by adopting a distributive economic system based on equity.

• "*Minimizing the use of natural resources*", which represents the principle of efficiency and the implementation

---

[98] OFSTAD, S., WESTLY, L., BRATELLI, T., Norway, Miljøverndepartementet, Symposium on Sustainable Consumption (Eds.), 1994. Symposium: sustainable consumption: 19-20 January 1994☐: Oslo, Norway. Ministry of Environment, Oslo, Norway.

of mechanisms to keep the products included in the value chain.

• reduce the use of "*toxic materials*", "*emissions of waste and pollutants*" to stimulate the regenerative factor of the circularity; and finally,

• the awareness about the intragenerational equity represented by the "*needs of future generations.*"

It is essential to reflect on the targets under SDG 12 To advance the understanding of the concept and formulate and assess strategies related to sustainable production and consumption.

The targets 12.1 and 12.A express the principle of common but differentiated responsibilities[99], attributing the implementation of programs on sustainable consumption and production[100] to all countries, and, at the same time,

---

[99] The principle of Common but Differentiated Responsibilities (CBDR) establishes that all nations shall cooperate to tackle global environmental degradation according to their economic and social development levels. The CBDR combines the ideal of the "common heritage of mankind" and the recognition of the world's asymmetries regarding accountability to contribute effectively to environmental protection and sustainable development. The CBDR presents a conceptual approach to understanding better and systematically analyzing the interactions among the natural environment, human activities, and political power by assigning greater responsibilities to developed nations that historically contribute most to the earth system's current state.

[100] Target 12.1 mentions the 10-Year Framework of Programs on Sustainable Consumption and Production Patterns (10YFP), which the United Conference on Sustainable Development adopted in 2012 (Rio+20). According to this program, "fundamental changes in how societies produce and consume are indispensable for achieving global sustainable development" (Johannesburg Plan of Implementation, 2002).

accounting for their lead to the developed nations. Considering their historical levels of development and scientific and technological capabilities, the developed nations can support the developing nations to move towards more sustainable patterns of consumption and production.

Through international cooperation to support capacity building and facilitate access to technical and financial assistance, both developed and developing countries can accelerate the shift towards sustainable consumption and production patterns and resource efficiency initiatives[101].

The programs, which are implemented by the Netherlands Enterprise Agency, are one example of how the

---

The framework will also stimulate innovation and cooperation to achieve a systemic collective impact towards SCP patterns.

[101] As previously discussed, the shift towards circularity holds the promise of a significant increase in job opportunities. This is due to the implementation of strategies aimed at enhancing the reuse and regeneration of products and materials. However, as highlighted in the report *Decent Work in the Circular Economy: An Overview of the Existing Evidence Base*, these prospects may encounter unique challenges in the Global South. The report underscores the need for more comprehensive research on the impact of circular economy interventions. It points out that current research on jobs in the circular economy often overlooks the effects on people in the Global South, atypical workers, women, migrants, youth, and other vulnerable populations. Addressing these gaps is crucial for more informed decision-making. The report concludes that research should strongly emphasize the Global South, informal workers, and global value chains. To better understand the principle of equity, more comprehensive and inclusive research on decent work and the circular economy is needed (CIRCLE ECONOMY. *Decent Work in the Circular Economy: An Overview of the Existing Evidence Base (joint report by Circle Economy, the International Labour Organization (ILO) and the Solutions for Youth Employment (S4YE) Programme of the World Bank)*. Available at: https://www.circle-economy.com/resources/decent-work-in-the-circular-economy).

principle of common but differentiated responsibilities is instrumentalized through international supply chains[102].

The Netherlands Enterprise Agency plays a pivotal role in encouraging companies to investigate and address human and environmental risks in their international value chains, such as child labor and poor working conditions, environmental pollution, and large-scale deforestation in developing nations.

The Netherlands Enterprise Agency is crucial in fostering sustainable and responsible value chains through various impactful subsidies and programs designed to benefit a business or organization significantly: Social Sustainability Fund (SSF); Sectoral Partnerships Pillar 1; European Partnership for Responsible Minerals (EPRM); Fund against Child Labour (FBK); Fund for Responsible Business (FVO).

These programs are initiatives designed to support projects and partnerships to make value chains in combination countries more sustainable through responsible business conduct, innovation, and market transformation, which are critical elements in this journey.

Targets 12.2 and 12.5 refer to the concept of sustainable production and consumption as a combination of efficient use of natural resources and waste management

---

[102] NETHERLANDS ENTERPRISE AGENCY. *Subsidy Guide*. Available at: https://english.rvo.nl/subsidy-guide.

(prevention, reduction, recycling, and reuse) that aim to implement governing practices through multiple collective actions to orientate them in a way that will preserve our planetary resources for the present and future generations[103].

Among the different definitions of waste, McKinney and Baran conceptualize waste as the product of a system's inefficiency caused by human activities and materials people want to dispose of[104].

Of course, as *"technical inefficiency,"* the idea of waste refers to a human-related value notion that could be perfectly transformed inside the logic of value creation in the circular economy and its replication of the natural system: *waste is food*.

Companies are now seeing waste as more than just a *"technical inefficiency"*, but as a potential business opportunity.

---

[103] Waste management refers to a governing process that aims to preserve the quality of life and human health and environmental protection through a sustainable management plan to progress on waste source reduction. Waste management can be recognized by the following characteristics: (a) collection, transport, treatment, and disposal of waste; (b) control, monitoring, and regulation of the production, collection, transport, treatment, and disposal of waste; and (c) prevention of waste production through in-process modifications, reuse, and recycling (Glossary of Environment Statistics, Studies in Methods, Series F, No. 67, United Nations, New York, 1997).

[104] PONGRÀCZ, E. et al. *Evolving the Theory of Waste Management: Defining key Concepts. Progress in Industrial Ecology*—An International Journal, 3, 59-74, 2004.

A sustainably driven company, Pela is leading the way by transforming the issue of plastic waste into a solution for consumers by offering a sustainable and accessible alternative to traditional plastic phone cases. Their cases, made of Flaxstic and compostable bioplastic elastomer, are not only eco-friendly but also durable and shock-absorbent.

It naturally appeals to consumers who wish to purchase eco-friendly phone case alternatives that will not damage the environment or contribute to the growing plastic waste. The sale of its cases prevented 966,739 pounds of plastic from flowing into the waste stream[105].

Pela has introduced *'Pela 360'*, a system that encourages customers to bring in their traditional plastic case when purchasing a Pela case. This ensures that 1 pound of plastic does not enter the waste stream. Under this system, the old plastic case is either upcycled into a new Pela case or properly recycled, further reducing the environmental impact of plastic waste. Pela aims to close the loop by upcycling the old plastic case into a new Pela case or ensuring that it is

---

[105] PELA CASE. *Our Story & Mission*. Available at: https://pelacase.com/pages/our-story. Pela's commitment to transparency and sustainability is not just a claim but a proven track record. They regularly publish their sustainable impact reports, disclose their donations to NGOs and for-profit organizations, and share their latest certifications. Their acquisition of the Climate Neutral certification, which holds them accountable for their greenhouse gas emissions, is a testament to their dedication. This transparency and dedication should reassure Pela's commitment to sustainable practices.

properly recycled. It is actively exploring innovative ways to further reduce their environmental footprint through design out waste from its operations.

Pela follows a basic circular business strategy: the product life extension (PLE) strategy. This strategy revolves around designing products that are built to be durable and eliminate the need for the consumer to re-purchase the product often. Another circular business strategy is applying the design for recycling strategy (DFR). This strategy revolves around designing products that aim for the highest level of recoverability of the materials used, thereby minimizing waste and maximizing resource efficiency.

Cities are also taking ambitious steps to implement innovative waste management methods and promote a circular economy in the public sphere. They see this as a catalyst for efficiency and innovation that can benefit various stakeholders, including citizens, producers, retailers, and service providers on both operational and strategic levels.[106].

Copenhagen is on a pioneering path to become the first carbon-neutral capital by 2025 and a global leader in urban circular economy. The innovative Circular Copenhagen Resource and Waste Plan, designed to address

---

[106] C40 CITIES and CLIMATE KIC. *Circular City Project. Municipality-led circular economy: Case Studies*. Available at: https://www.climate-kic.org/wp-content/uploads/sites/15/2018/12/Municipality-led-circular-economy-case-studies-compressed-ilovepdf-compressed.pdf.

municipal waste from households and the light industry, is a testament to this vision. The plan's ambitious goal to recycle 70% of municipal waste by 2024 will significantly reduce 59,000 tons of CO_2 per year.

The plan includes specific actions focused on various themes, such as conducting an information campaign on waste sorting, enhancing waste collection methods, introducing source separation, incorporating new technology for waste treatment, and encouraging a circular economy. This approach aims to increase household waste recycling by 29% and provide economic benefits to the city and its residents, including job creation and reduced environmental impact.

Another crucial aspect of the plan is its emphasis on collaboration and innovation. The plan aims to stimulate innovation and provide a testing facility for sorting plastics by bringing together innovative businesses, researchers, and industry professionals through a dedicated platform.

The city is dedicated to testing new waste collection methods. By utilizing electric vehicles to reduce noise and air emissions, the city is taking a significant step toward becoming carbon-neutral by 2025. These efforts to replace trucks running on natural gas or biogas reaffirm the city's commitment to a greener community[107].

---

[107] C40 CITIES. *Circular Copenhagen – 70 % Waste Recycled by 2024.*

Target 12.4 aims to achieve environmentally sound management of chemicals and all waste throughout their life cycle and mitigate their release to air, water, and soil. These practices shall respect agreed international frameworks and reduce negative impacts on human health and the environment[108].

Available at: https://www.c40.org/case-studies/circular-copenhagen-70-waste-recycled-by-2024/. Here, it is relevant to mention the C40 Cities, a global network that connects nearly 100 mayors to act against climate change through an inclusive, science-based, and collaborative approach. The goal is to cut their fair share of emissions in half by 2030, help the world limit global warming to 1.5°C, and build healthy, equitable, and resilient communities. C40 cities are committed to delivering on the most ambitious goals of the Paris Agreement at the local level, supporting its members in multiple ways, such as facilitating access to finance for investments in green jobs and projects that improve city resilience, scaling up climate action, and sharing best practices across high-impact sectors.

[108] One of the international agreements mentioned in Target 12.4 is the Stockholm Convention on Persistent Organic Pollutants (POPs), which became effective on May 17, 2004; it is a global treaty aimed at safeguarding human health and the environment by restricting and ultimately eliminating the production, use, trade, release, and storage of hazardous, long-lasting chemicals. The Stockholm Convention is a legally binding international instrument designed to gradually reduce the presence of persistent organic pollutants in the environment. Although successful in identifying new POPs, its implementation at the national level remains challenging, especially for low- and middle-income countries. Persistent Organic Pollutants (POPs) have been proven to have negative effects on human health and the environment. The Stockholm Convention addresses a group of 12 highly persistent and toxic chemicals, including aldrin, chlordane, DDT, dieldrin, endrin, heptachlor, hexachlorobenzene, mirex, polychlorinated biphenyls, polychlorinated dibenzo-p-dioxins, polychlorinated dibenzofurans, and toxaphene. Another critical international agreement is the Basel Convention on the Control of Transboundary Movements of Hazardous Wastes and their Disposal, which was adopted in 1989 and entered into force in 1992. It aims to reduce the movement of hazardous waste between nations, particularly from developed to less developed countries (LDCs). The

In accordance with target 12.4, the European Green Deal's zero pollution ambition for 2050[109] includes the Chemicals Strategy for Sustainability (CSS). This strategy not only aims to prevent harm to people and the environment from hazardous chemicals but also plays a crucial role in supporting EU industry innovation by promoting the use of safer and more sustainable chemicals[110].

One critical sector notorious for its excessive water and chemical usage and the resulting toxic waste is the textile industry. This represents a pressing issue, particularly in countries like China, India, Bangladesh, Vietnam, and Thailand. In this field, the private sector has made a significant global impact through innovative technological processes, as demonstrated by the Dutch company DyeCoo[111].

Basel Convention is guided by principles that focus on reducing hazardous waste generation and transboundary movements. These principles stress the significance of managing hazardous wastes in an environmentally sound manner, treating, and disposing of them as close as possible to their generation source, and minimizing them at the source.

[109] The zero pollution vision for 2050 aims to reduce air, water, and soil pollution to levels that are no longer considered harmful to human health and natural ecosystems. This long-term vision respects the boundaries our planet can cope with and ultimately strives to create a toxic-free environment.

[110] On 25th April 2022, the European Commission demonstrated its commitment to reducing harmful substances by publishing a comprehensive Restrictions Roadmap under the CSS. This roadmap outlines restrictions for the most harmful substances to human health and the environment, including carcinogenic, mutagenic, and reprotoxic substances (CMRs), endocrine disruptors, persistent, bioaccumulative, and toxic (PBT) and very persistent and very bioaccumulative (vPvB) substances, immunotoxicants, neurotoxicants, substances harmful to specific organs, and respiratory sensitizers for all uses.

DyeCoo uses a highly pressurized form of carbon dioxide known as 'supercritical' carbon dioxide. This unique state of carbon dioxide, which is halfway between a liquid and a gas, allows it to dissolve the dye and carry it deep into the fabric. The process does not require additional chemicals or water. Once the dye is dissolved, the carbon dioxide evaporates and is then recycled and used again, making it a closed-loop system[112].

DyeCoo's method is not only environmentally friendly but also cost-effective. The process eliminates the need for large amounts of water and chemicals, reducing operational costs. Additionally, the high absorption rate of the dye and the reduced drying time significantly increase production efficiency, leading to cost savings[113].

Concerns about food security[114] and circularity are revealed by target 12.3, which aims to halve per capita global

---

[111] DYECOO. Available at: https://dyecoo.com/dyecoo/

[112] WORLD ECONOMIC FORUM. *Open Up a Sustainable Wardrobe*. Available at: https://wef.ch/353dYI7 #sdi19 #sustainableworld.

[113] The unique process of DyeCoo results in 98% of the dye being absorbed by the cloth, creating an eco-friendly product. This high absorption rate not only reduces waste but also minimizes the need for drying, cutting production time in half and significantly reducing energy consumption. The company's successful partnerships with major brands like Nike and IKEA, who have seen significant cost reductions, are a testament to its effectiveness and financial viability.

[114] The Food and Agriculture Organization of the UN provides the definition of a state of food security: *"Food security exists when all people, at all times, have physical, social and economic access to sufficient, safe and nutritious food which meets their dietary needs and food preferences for an active and healthy life"*. Food security is

food waste at the retail and consumer levels and reduce food losses along production and supply chains, including post-harvest losses[115].

This target is linked to the general framework of zero hunger (SDG 2). It focuses on food availability and its supply chain: production, distribution, and exchange to ensure enough and appropriate quality food at a given time.

The Food Loss & Waste Protocol is a global multistakeholder partnership that represents the international effort to reduce food waste. It is led by a Steering Committee composed of seven expert institutions[116].

In 2016, the partnership developed the Food Loss and Waste Accounting and Reporting Standard (the FLW

---

generally understood to incorporate four main components: availability, access, utilization, and stability. All these components must be sufficiently present to achieve a state of food security.

[115] Food loss or waste is a significant challenge that requires the attention and action of policymakers and food industry professionals. The scale of this problem is best understood through its multiple impacts. Approximately one-third of all food produced in the world is lost or wasted, resulting in significant economic losses globally, estimated at around $940 billion per year. This inefficiency also contributes to increased food insecurity, hinders nutrition, and has serious environmental impacts. It consumes about one-quarter of all water used by agriculture each year, requires land area greater than the size of China, and generates about 8 percent of global greenhouse gas emissions annually (FOOD AND AGRICULTURE ORGANIZATION. *Food Wastage Footprint & Climate Change*. Rome: UN FAO, 2015).

[116] The Steering Committee comprises the Consumer Goods Forum (CGF), the Food and Agriculture Organization of the United Nations (FAO), EU-FUSIONS, the United Nations Environment Programme, the World Business Council for Sustainable Development (WBCSD), the Waste & Resources Action Programme (WRAP), and the World Resources Institute (WRI), with WRI serving as the Secretariat.

Standard) to assist companies, countries, and other stakeholders in understanding the quantity, location, and causes of food loss and waste within borders, operations, or supply chains. This information enables them to measure and effectively help decision-makers better understand and manage how much, where, and why food is being lost or wasted[117].

The government of the state of Oregon (US) initiated the "*Wasted Food Measurement Study*" as part of its commitment to reduce food waste by 50 percent by 2030, based on the FLWS. The study monitored food wastage in urban and rural households using quantitative and qualitative research methods to gain insights into the amount, type, and reasons citizens discarded food. The study yielded the following key findings:

- Of all food waste thrown away by households, 71 percent could have been eaten (i.e., it was not bones, shells, peels, etc.)

---

[117] The global standard is a powerful tool, designed to provide practical inventory based on specific quantification goals. By using precise terminology and requirements, it ensures international consistency, enables comprehensiveness, facilitates comparability, and supports transparency. Quantifying food loss and waste is not just a technical exercise. It's a strategic move that can lead to significant benefits, such as reducing costs associated with over-purchasing and disposal, avoiding greenhouse gas emissions, and supporting efforts to eliminate hunger.

- On average, Oregon households throw away 6.3 pounds of food per week (or 2.3 pounds per capita).
- Fruits and vegetables are the most commonly discarded food that could have been eaten.
- There were no significant differences in the amounts of wasted food generated among demographic groups, such as household size or type, urban or rural, or income level.
- The top three loss reasons for throwing away food were: 1) food is moldy or spoiled, 2) household members didn'tlike or were tired of eating a food, and 3) food was not good as leftovers[118].

According to the World Business Council for Sustainable Development, the FLW Standard facilitates consistent baseline measurement and tracking of progress towards Target 12.3. It promotes consistency and transparency in quantifying and reporting food loss and waste. More than that, it seeks to inspire and empower countries, companies, and other entities to act and minimize food loss and waste. This empowerment can lead to significant economic benefits, improved food security,

---

[118] DEPARTMENT OF ENVIRONMENTAL QUALITY. STATE OF OREGON. Wasted Food Measurement Study: Oregon Households. Available at: https://www.oregon.gov/deq/mm/food/Pages/Wasted-Food-Study.aspx

enhanced natural resource use efficiency, and reduced environmental impacts[119].

From the private sector perspective, with a pioneering spirit, Toast Ale, a company founded in 2015 in London, has taken a novel approach to combatting food waste and the climate crisis. Instead of contributing to the problem, they use surplus bread from bakeries and sandwich makers to replace barley in their beer, a genuinely innovative solution[120].

The company buys excess bakery bread and heel ends from sandwich makers and uses them to replace 25% of the malted barley in all its beers. Using a surplus ingredient not only prevents waste but also implies less malted barley and, so, less of nature's resources to produce it—less land, less water, and less energy, resulting in fewer carbon emissions.

Toast Ale has saved over 2 million slices of bread, cut 42 tons of CO2 emissions, reclaimed 175 553 m2 of land, and saved over 250 litres of water. Beyond the environmental impact, Toast Ale donated over 48000$ to charity to help fix the food system and fight food waste. By saving up to a slice

---

[119] WORLD BUSINESS COUNCIL FOR SUSTAINABLE DEVELOPMENT (WBCSD). *Food Loss and Waste Accounting and Reporting Standard*. Available at: https://www.wbcsd.org/resources/food-loss-and-waste-accounting-and-reporting-standard-2/

[120] TOAST ALE. *Sustainability*. Available at: https://www.toastbrewing.com/sustainability.

of bread per bottle, Toast Ales inspires a collective effort for a more circular and healthier planet.

Businesses are called to adopt sustainable practices and integrate sustainability information into their reporting cycle at the target 12.6. By encouraging businesses to use sustainable practices approaches based on a "closed-loop" supply chain to maintain and recover value from products at their highest utility while contributing to designing out waste, this target aims to accelerate the transition from linear to circular economy, contributing to the implementation of efficient supply chains and innovative methods to respond to hyper-consumption and minimized environmental footprint.

Some strategies companies adopt to integrate the circular mindset in their operations are not just theoretical concepts. They involve practical steps such as retaining product ownership, extending the product life cycle, and eco-friendly design. These strategies are part of the overall approach of this book, which are extensively discussed in this Chapter (Item 3.2, *Circular Strategies*), and Chapter 5 (Item 5.2, *Circular Business Strategies*).

Regarding reporting and communication, EU companies must publicly disclose detailed information on how they operate and manage social and environmental risks, as the European Commission approved its proposal for the Corporate Sustainability Reporting Directive (CSRD).

From January 2024, Member States of the EU must enforce the CSRD and its requirements to hold businesses more accountable for their impact on people and the planet while giving investors and the public access to comparable, reliable, and easily accessible information on sustainability.

The CSRD set up mandatory company guidelines and standards based on the European Sustainability Reporting Standards (ESRS). These guidelines, to be included in annual management reports, aim to streamline reporting processes and enhance transparency. The implementation timelines, tailored to the company's size, provide a structured path for adaptation. This mandatory directive is a crucial aspect of the European Green Deal, which requires EU companies to significantly adapt their strategies, operations, and value chains[121].

Target 12.7 involves the concept of circular procurement that consists of the act of buying products and services complying with environmental and social standards. It requires defining and fulfilling a need while following the principles of circularity. This involves re-evaluating requirements, criteria, contract strategies, business models, and internal practices to minimize the use of new materials,

---

[121] The CSRD attempts to create a roadmap for a significant contribution to sustainability by broadening the range of organizations subject to regulation, establishing consistent reporting criteria, and improving sustainability disclosures' overall quality and comparability to enhance transparency, accountability, and coordinating efforts.

reduce waste, and establish closed-loop systems that benefit the environment and society.

In 2019, the Agency for Facility Operations of the Flemish Government implemented a new framework contract for office furniture based on circular procurement. The contract includes a solution where the supplier manages the furniture needs of the government's different entities and offices in various locations through a credit scheme.

When government organizations have surplus furniture, they return it to the system for reuse. As a reward, they receive a credit that can be used to purchase other furniture from the supplier's web shop of reused furniture, demonstrating a strategy focused on resource efficiency. This not only promotes circularity but also ensures a cost-effective solution for the government's furniture needs[122].

Implementing circular procurement offers substantial benefits in a business setting. Its goal is to minimize negative impacts and yield positive outcomes by eliminating hazardous materials and waste from the supply chain and carefully choosing suppliers with fair labour practices. This approach reduces environmental harm and bolsters the

---

[122] PROCIRC. Pilot Projects: *Attractive refurbished furniture in Government of Flanders' offices.* Available at: https://northsearegion.eu/procirc/pilot-projects/attractive-refurbished-furniture-in-government-of-flanders-offices/.

company's reputation and relationships with suppliers through long-term partnerships.

IKEA is recognized worldwide for its efforts to achieve sustainability throughout its supply chain. The company sources almost half of its wood from sustainable forests, and the same is true for its cotton suppliers, who follow the Better Cotton Standards, which minimize water pollution through organic farming practices[123]. Additionally, the use of pesticides and chemical fertilizers is regulated.

IWAY is the IKEA way of responsibly procuring products, services, materials, and components. It sets clear expectations and ways of working to improve environmental impacts, secure decent and meaningful work, respect children's rights, and improve the welfare of animals in the IKEA value chain. This initiative demonstrates a requirement for all suppliers and service providers working with IKEA

---

[123] In line with the SDGs, the Better Cotton Standard aims to establish a holistic system for sustainable cotton production. This is achieved through the practice of regenerative agriculture, which involves restoring and replenishing the soil, rather than depleting it, and promoting biodiversity. The standard also encourages the exchange of best practices and stimulating collective action in terms of decent work, reducing inequalities, and gender empowerment to convert cotton into a sustainable mainstream commodity and impact lives and livelihoods. The Better Cotton Standard is not just a set of rules, but a collaborative effort. It is supported by critical principles involving capacity building, connections, compliance, monitoring, and measuring progress. Each of these principles plays a crucial role in the collective journey toward sustainable cotton production, highlighting the value placed on every stakeholder's contribution.

and a shared commitment, underlining their joint dedication to enhancing circular practices[124].

Raising awareness and transparency are the fundamental ideas of target 12.8 to stimulate sustainable lifestyles in harmony with nature. Kaptein and Van Tulder affirmed that transparency provides information to stakeholders to give them proper insight into the relevant issues[125].

Transparent information and awareness about sustainable development and circularity can promote individual and social lifestyles to mitigate the use of our planet's finite natural resources, educate people about environmental protection, and understand their interaction with nature.

One example of the application of this target is the so-called Brand Activism. Driven by a sense of justice, brand activism refers to business efforts to affect and raise public awareness by sharing its position about problems that concern society, with the goal of making a positive impact on the world[126].

---

[124] IKEA. *IWAY: the IKEA Supplier Code of Conduct.* Available at: https://www.ikea.com/global/en/our-business/how-we-work/iway-our-supplier-code-of-conduct/.

[125] KAPTEIN, M. and VAN TULDER, R. *Toward Effective Stakeholder Dialogue*, Business and Society Review, 108:2, 203-224, 2003.

[126] It's important to note that brand activism can also be risky. It may alienate certain customer segments or attract backlash from those who disagree with the brand's stance. Brand activism can be planned, allowing

For instance, Ben & Jerry's has been a strong advocate for climate justice. For years, the company has supported activists fighting for climate justice, answering one simple question: "*Can ice cream help save the world? We think so*".

They have infused their ice cream flavors with powerful messages, in line with a global movement to support farmers and all frontline communities. Their commitment is unwavering as they stand with those most vulnerable to the unpredictable and extreme weather and global market disruptions caused by climate change.

[127]

---

brands to include the message in their marketing campaigns to build operations around it. On the other hand, it can also be reactive, responding to real-time events. This agile approach allows brands to stay relevant and engage with their audience in a dynamic, ever-changing world.

[127] BEN & JERRY'S. *Ben & Jerry's Is Fighting for Climate Justice, One Scoop at a Time*. Available at: https://www.benjerry.com/whats-new/2021/10/ben-jerrys-fighting-for-climate-justice. They have partnered with Fairtrade through their Producer Development Initiative Fund,

The company is dedicated to reducing greenhouse gas emissions from dairy by more than half in the next decade. Additionally, they are assisting farmers in adopting agricultural practices that will improve the health of their cows, make their soil more productive, and enhance their standard of living. This support is provided by paying an extra social premium on top of the purchase price of their crop.

Target 12. B reveals concerns related to a specific sector: tourism in which sustainability has emerged as a core aspect of most activities. This target aims to develop and implement tools to monitor sustainable tourism that creates jobs and promotes local culture and products.

According to the United Nations World Tourism Organization (UNWTO), a circular strategy to develop and implement sustainable tourism patterns involves using environmental resources to protect essential ecological processes and conserve natural heritage and biodiversity. It is also relevant to respect the socio-cultural authenticity of host communities, conserve their built and living cultural heritage

---

providing extra funding and resources to enhance climate resilience. This includes initiatives such as agroforestry and irrigation, which benefit rural communities. In November 2020, they pledged to pay a higher price, in addition to the existing Fairtrade premium, to support cocoa farmers in the Ivory Coast in achieving a living income.

and traditional values, and contribute to intercultural understanding and tolerance.

Finally, this strategy is completed by ensuring viable, long-term economic operations, providing socio-economic benefits to all stakeholders that are fairly distributed, including stable employment and income-earning opportunities and social services to host communities, and contributing to poverty alleviation[128].

The One Planet Sustainable Tourism Program promotes sustainable consumption and production (SCP) in the tourism sector. It focuses on implementing SDG 12 by addressing climate change, pollution, and biodiversity loss through tourism policies and practices. The program also advocates integrating circular economy principles and practices to decouple tourism operations from environmental degradation and enhance resilience.

UNWTO has led the implementation of the Program, supporting the translation of SCP's complexity into actionable areas for tourism stakeholders. This initiative added value to over 700 members and generated dialogue between the environment and tourism stakeholders[129].

---

[128] UNITED NATIONS WORLD TOURISM ORGANIZATION. *Definition of Sustainable Tourism*. Available at: https://www.unwto.org/sustainable-development.

[129] The One Planet Sustainable Tourism Programme is a multi-stakeholder partnership that promotes knowledge sharing and networking and provides guidance to address collective priorities. The program

As part of the One Planet Sustainable Tourism Program, the Abu Dhabi Premier Inn has partnered with Waterscan, a water treatment expert, to implement the region's first water recycling system. This system significantly reduces the hotel's water consumption, saving an average of 735,000 liters of water per month, which is approximately a quarter of the hotel's monthly water usage.

The Waterscan system operates by collecting wastewater from bathing and showering in the hotel's 300 rooms. This water is then meticulously filtered using an ultra-filtration membrane. The purified water is then returned for use in irrigating and flushing toilets, effectively reducing the hotel's water consumption by 60 liters per guest[130].

Target 12.C is about circularity and rationalizing the inefficient fossil-fuel subsidies that encourage wasteful consumption. It considers the specific needs and conditions of developing countries and minimizes the possible adverse impacts on their development. Importantly, it does so in a

---

currently focuses on three main areas of intervention: 1. Accelerating climate action; 2. Building a circular economy of plastics; 3. Transforming food value chains (UNITED NATIONS WORLD TOURISM ORGANIZATION. *The One Planet Sustainable Tourism Programme*. Available at: https://www.unwto.org/sustainable-development/one-planet).

[130] ONE PLANET NETWROK. *Case Studies: Innovative Greywater Recycling in Hotels: Abu Dhabi Premier Inn*. Available at: https://www.oneplanetnetwork.org/knowledge.centre/resources/innovative-greywater-recycling-hotels.

manner that protects people with low incomes and the affected communities.

Inefficient subsidies for fossil fuels, such as tax breaks for oil companies, undermine governments' ability to achieve circular goals. They often disproportionately benefit wealthier segments of the population, leading to increased poverty and inequalities.

For instance, these subsidies could be used to fund social welfare programs or education, which would benefit a wider range of people and reduce inequality. This violation of the principle of equity is a significant concern in the energy sector.

This goal is important because it generates accurate and high-quality data to map current subsidies from consumers and producers. This will improve transparency and help in making informed decisions based on national and global trends, allowing for the development of policies related to repurposing and reforming the energy sector.

The significance of target 12.C can be understood by examining the current strategies adopted by the International Energy Agency (IEA), which was established in 1974 to coordinate responses to major oil supply disruptions.

Since 2015, the agency has broadened its focus to encompass energy security in natural gas and electricity sectors. Additionally, it has become a center for clean-energy technologies and energy efficiency, placing strong emphasis on advancing global progress towards sustainable goals.

As part of its evolution, the agency has implemented mechanisms to assess fossil fuel subsidies. These assessments are included in the World Energy Outlook, providing vital information for policymakers, energy markets, and consumers to support their decision-making.

Effectively reallocating fossil fuel subsidies to other development strategies and social supports, such as renewable energy projects or public transportation, enables comprehensive tracking of market tendencies.

By redirecting these funds, we can observe shifts in consumer behavior and market demand, paving the way for a more sustainable and circular energy system. This shift can guide energy interventions prioritizing sustainability and circularity, offering a hopeful outlook for environmental regeneration and social inclusion.

The circular mindset involves using renewable sources of energy that are naturally replenished on a human timescale and can never be depleted, such as sunlight, wind, hydropower, geothermal heat, and biomass.

These energy sources not only do not harm the environment, like pumping GHGs into the atmosphere, but they also play a crucial role in providing the necessary time for ecosystems to replenish themselves, thereby maintaining a balanced and healthy environment[131].

The analysis of the targets of SDG 12 underscores the complexities involved in progressing toward circularity and their potential as strategies to tackle wicked problems. The circular transition necessitates engagement from a multitude of stakeholders. The case studies described in this topic demonstrate the active involvement of various entities and their efforts in incorporating circular practices in their operations.

These case studies, which range from public to private institutions, the establishment of norms and regulations, and the formation of partnerships, reveal a series of governing arrangements characterized by innovation, cooperation, and complexity. They also stress the importance of full cooperation and solidarity through collective effort in building circularity.

---

[131] According to Bocken et al., strategies that narrow, slow, and close resource loops to achieve environmental, social, and economic goals demonstrate the connection between renewable energy technologies and circularity. However, designing technology for the circular economy is challenging. It requires a better comprehension of resources and material options, optimizing their performance, and finding end-of-life solutions to identify the most appropriate life cycle management strategies (BOCKEN, N.M.P., DE PAUW, I., BAKKER, C., VAN DER GRINTEN, B. *Product design and business model strategies for a circular economy*. In: Journal of Industrial Production and Engineering 33(5): 308-320, 2016).

4. HYPER-CONSUMPTION AND CIRCULARITY: PLANNED OBSOLESCENCE

4.1. Hyper-Consumption

In simple terms, consumption refers to the use of goods and services or the amount of goods and services used to meet our needs and desires. Given its impact on the environment, society, and quality of life, consumption is closely linked to the concept of circularity, which aims to promote balanced lifestyles within the Earth's limited resources.

The traditional school of economics, as exemplified by Keynesian theory, sees consumption as the driving force behind an economy's income and output. Changes in production are influenced by the demand for goods and services. A decrease in production can set off a chain reaction, affecting business profits and leading to unemployment. This demonstrates the complex interconnections among production, consumption, and employment.

In his book Design for Business (1947), Gordon Lippincott revealed that the significant problem for manufacturers and designers was continually *"stimulating the urge to buy"*. This idea represented the standard in a market economy in the second half of the last century, which was based on conspicuous consumption: *"Any method that can motivate the flow of merchandise to new buyers will create jobs and work for industry, and hence national prosperity (...) Our custom of trading in our automobiles every year, of having a new refrigerator, vacuum cleaner or electric iron every three or four years is economically sound"*[132].

However, the consumption patterns developed in the 20th century have become unsustainable today, particularly for our ecosystems, social equality, and well-being. Currently, consumption has become consumerism (or hyper-consumption), which encourages the acquisition of goods and services in ever-increasing quantities.[133].

Zygmunt Bauman argues that today, people's identities have become closely linked to consumerism: *"an activity shaped in the likeness of shopping"*. Shopping has become an integral part of our lifestyle, emphasizing the constant pursuit of new purchases. This has led to a situation where the value we place on our lives is often tied to the

---

[132] LIPPINCOTT, J. G., *Design for Business*, p. 14. Chicago: P. Theobald Publishers, 1947.

[133] Gilles Lipovetsky stated that, since the second half of the 20th century, our society has been converted into a "hyper-consumption society" because it considers itself *"a vehicle for a veritable explosion of individualism, a hyper-individualism; with multi-equipment allowing independent activities, individualized consumerism, personalized use of space, time and goods"* (LIPOVETSKY, G. *The Hyperconsumption Society*, p. 27. In Beyond Consumption Bubble. Edited by Karin Elström and Kays Glans. Routledge, 2011).

material goods and services we consume rather than the human values that should define and enrich us[134].

In the past, consumption was primarily about survival or comfort. In our modern society, however, the culture of consumption is so pervasive that people organize their lives around the acquisition and use of consumer goods and services, using them to shape their sense of identity and purpose.

Today, consumption has become an end in itself: people conspicuously consume, without any restriction or constraint, to seek a specific type of emotional satisfaction that causes them the sensation of happiness. This shift in the culture of consumption has profound implications for our society, influencing everything from our economy to our social interactions.

Maslow's pyramid clearly explains this situation by listing human needs in a hierarchical order, starting from basic physiological needs (such as food, water, sex, and sleep) and safety needs (related to health, family, property, etc.) to those associated with self-actualization (morality, creativity, spontaneity, etc.). These needs must be fulfilled at each level before progressing to the next higher level.[135].

---

[134] BAUMAN, Z. *Liquid Modernity*. Blackwell Publishing, 2006.
[135] Maslow's hierarchy provides a better comprehension of consumer behavior, as it explains how purchasing decisions are prioritized according to their needs. In a simple illustration, a hungry consumer will prioritize buying food over luxury items. Based on Maslow's framework,

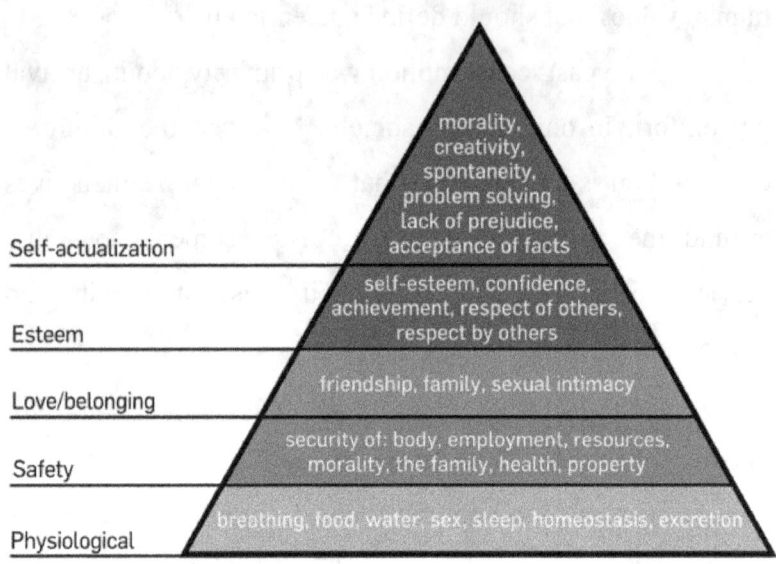

Our modern lifestyle has shifted our focus from the fundamental need to protect ourselves to the esteem to gain respect and social status through consumption rather than genuine esteem for others and being respected by others.

Of course, consumption plays a vital role in innovation and creativity. However, its side effects are more dangerous for humanity and its social relationships with the environment, affecting our empathy with the planet and its other living species.

---

businesses can elaborate marketing strategies oriented to consumers' needs by identifying target markets and offering tailored products or services.

This complex process requires considerable effort to transform ourselves into excellent consumers, to seek esteem in shopping, and to move away from our tendencies to adopt a solitary lifestyle as a form of self-actualization, the last segment of Maslow's pyramid. This lifestyle prioritizes simple human values and social relationships over material possessions.

Dimitrova, Ilieva, and Stanev formulated an exciting allusion to Descartes to explain the effects of hyper-consumption nowadays: *"It seems that Descartes' famous maxim 'I think, therefore I am' has been transformed into 'I consume, therefore I am'", presenting the newest version of the Cartesian understanding of existence"*[136].

This dynamic, a result of the linear paradigm's relentless cycle of *"new needs and unlimited wants"*, compels businesses to increase sales by cutting costs. It fosters in consumers a craving for products with short life cycles, leading them to constantly pursue the latest versions, even if their current ones are perfectly functional.

As Weetman states, the impact of "the striving for consumption" can cause dangerous climate change by burning fossil fuels, using fertilizers, and clearing forests, all

---

[136] DIMITROVA, T., ILIEVA, I., and STANEV, V. *I Consume, Therefore I Am? Hyperconsumption Behavior: Scale Development and Validation.* Social Sciences 11: 532, 2022. https://doi.org/10.3390/socsci11110532

of which create greenhouse gas (GHG) emissions. People have more money to spend on food, clothing, and other stuff. She concludes by affirming that it is great news that people's living standards are improving, but the downside is that we are creating more resource demand[137].

Rachel Botsman and Roo Rogers argue that we have overlooked the negative impacts of modern consumerism for too long. Over the last fifty years, we have consumed more goods and services than all previous generations combined. Modern capitalist society's endless pressure to acquire more and more stuff in increasingly large quantities is known as hyper-consumerism or hyper-consumption[138].

Frenchy Lunning defines hyper-consumption briefly as "*consumerism for the sake of consuming*"[139]. It involves using goods for non-functional purposes, such as buying a

---

[137] WEETMAN, C. *A Circular Economy Handbook: How to Build a More Resilient, Competitive and Sustainable Business.* Kogan Page, 2020. In a similar vein, but with a more critical perspective, mainly focusing on the principles of sufficiency and equity, Clair Brown explains that our materialistic and wasteful carbon-based global economy has resulted in significant inequality. This has led to luxurious lifestyles for those at the top and desperate lives for those at the bottom. Brown emphasizes the need for a collective effort to redirect our relentless pursuit of economic growth and consumption toward a more sustainable path. This path should not exploit the environment and harm the earth, our common home (BROWN, C. *Buddhist Economics: An Enlightened Approach to the Dismal Science*, p. 131. New York: Bloomsbury Press, 2017).
[138] BOTSMAN, R and ROGERS, R. *What's Mine is Yours? The Rise of Collaborative Consumption.* HarperCollins, 2010.
[139] LUNNING, F. *Fanthropologies*. U of Minnesota Press. pp. 140, 2010.

new phone when the current one is still functional or purchasing clothes for the sake of fashion rather than necessity. It is driven by the belief that material possessions define one's identity and contribute to personal well-being and happiness.

In this logic, the devotion to consumption is exemplary, and more consumption is even better. Therefore, hyper-consumption proposes an incessant race towards "novelty," stimulating consumers to acquire new goods and throw the old ones away, affecting the lifecycle of products that must be short to keep people purchasing more and more things in line with the values proposed by the linear economic system through planned obsolescence.

4.2. Planned Obsolescence

The concept of planned obsolescence becomes clear when we look at its historical development. In the early 20th century, when electricity was becoming widely adopted, manufacturers competed to create long-lasting light bulbs. However, this approach decreased the manufacturers' profits as consumers did not need to buy light bulbs frequently.

Therefore, they decided to create a worldwide cartel, known as Phoebus, to set prices and deliberately reduce the lifespan of their products, forcing consumers to purchase new bulbs regularly and increasing their sales[140]. Since then, this deliberate strategy, known as planned obsolescence, has been incorporated into nearly every existing product[141].

Obsolescence means going out of use, reflecting the idea of being irrelevant, useless, and outdated. When a product is considered obsolete, it will be replaced by new ones. This scheme is where planned obsolescence comes into play.

Planned obsolescence consists of intentionally designing products, ensuring they will become outdated, unwanted, or unusable within a specific time frame. This strategy ensures that consumers will replace obsolete products with new ones, encouraging purchasing, production, and more waste. Kamila Pope conceptualizes planned obsolescence as the artificial reduction of the durability of consumer goods to induce consumers to purchase substitute

---

[140] DANNORITZER, C et al. *The Lightbulb Conspiracy: The untold story of planned obsolescence* (video project), San Francisco, 2011.

[141] Jonker et al. analyze the historical process of creating the 'law of obsolescence,' a fundamental principle of our modern economy. This principle dictates that growth is achieved through increased production, sales, and consumption. It operates within a framework of intentionally shortening product lifecycles and making repair unprofitable. This systematic strategy results in a significant waste of materials and products, raising alarms about the environmental impact of obsolescence. The authors argue that obsolescence has permeated every aspect of our economy, from design and production cycles to organizational operations and macroeconomic indicators like Gross Domestic Product (GDP). (JONKER et al. *The Circular Economy: Developments, Concepts, and Research in Search for Corresponding Business Models*. Nijmegen: Radboud University, 2017).

products before they need to and, therefore, more often than they usually would [142].

Annie Leonard, from *"The Story of Stuff Project"* openly defined planned obsolescence as "*design for the dump*" which means creating products intended to be thrown away quickly. Using electronics as an example, she argued that they are difficult to upgrade, easy to break, and impractical to repair, forcing consumers to purchase new ones.

Products can be intentionally designed to become obsolete either by having limited functionality, such as a disposable paper coffee cup or a machine with easily breakable parts or by being made desirable for only a short period, like a piece of clothing that is fashionable for one year and then replaced by something else the next year[143].

In his classic book *"The Waste Makers"* (1960), Vance Packard analyzed the three different ways that products can be made obsolescent: *"Obsolescence of function. In this situation, an existing product becomes outmoded when a product is introduced that performs the function better. Obsolescence of quality. Here, when it is planned, a product breaks down or wears out at a given time,*

---

[142] POPE, K. *Understanding Planned Obsolescence: Unsustainability Through Production, Consumption and Waste Generation*, Kogan Page, 2017.
[143] LEONARD, A. *The Story of Electronics: Annotated Script*, 2020. https://www.storyofstuff.org/wp-content/uploads/2020/01/SoElectronics

usually not too distant. Obsolescence of desirability. In this situation, a product that is still sound in terms of quality or performance becomes "worn out" in our minds because a styling or other change makes it seem less desirable[144].

According to Packard's classification, functional obsolescence in the technology industry can be seen in the constant evolution of smartphones. New models offer more features, rendering old ones functionally outdated.

In the same sector, it is possible to illustrate the obsolescence of quality. For example, smartphones or laptops use non-replaceable batteries that degrade over time, causing a deterioration in performance. This means consumers cannot directly remove this part. The cost of replacing it with a technical service often leads to considering buying a new product.

In the clothing industry, obsolescence of quality can also be visualized, as nylon stockings are likely to snag, snare, or run, requiring regular replacement.

Finally, obsolescence of desirability, also known as perceived obsolescence, is less concerned with the functional or qualitative aspects of the product, but rather focuses on its style to align with market trends.

---

[144] PACKARD, V. The Waste Makers, David McKay Company, New York, 1960.

For instance, with the introduction of touch-screen phones, traditional button-operated mobile phones may seem outdated and lacking in style despite their functionality. This perceived obsolescence strategy influences customers to perceive themselves as *"uncool"* and *"outdated"*, compelling them always to purchase the latest version[145]. As a result, their self-esteem and identity become tied to material possessions and following trends, as previously analyzed using Maslow's pyramid of needs.

Bisschop, Hendlin, and Jaspers explained that perceived obsolescence, also known as style or psychological obsolescence, occurs when consumers feel the need to replace products for fashion, aesthetic, or status reasons, even if the products still work perfectly well[146].

New product lines are introduced more frequently, often with minor improvements, such as in aesthetics. This

---

[145] Another compelling example is a football team that subtly changes its kit design for the new season, exerting significant pressure on supporters who do not want to be seen in last season's shirt. The perception is that a supporter wearing the old shirt is seen as less committed than one wearing the new shirt. This marketing strategy emphasizes the significance of wearing the latest shirt as a symbol of loyalty and commitment. It does so to generate a sense of inclusion and identity, making the supporters feel part of a larger community and reinforcing their identity as a fan of the team. An out-of-date football shirt in a crowd of supporters wearing the new version subtly exerts social pressure, displacing those without and compelling them to purchase the latest version, even if it is only slightly different from last season's.

[146] BISSCHOP, L., HENDLIN, Y. & JASPERS, J. Designed to break: planned obsolescence as corporate environmental crime. *Crime Law Soc Change* **78**, 271–293. https://doi.org/10.1007/s10611-022-10023-4, 2022.

frequent introduction of new products is crucial for generating a short period of exposure, but it is enough to stimulate consumers' desire to purchase them.

4.2.1. Fast Fashion

Fashion is a global industry estimated at USD 1.3 trillion and employs around 300 million people along the value chain. However, it is also one of the most environmentally harmful industries in the world, ranking among the top 10 industries in countries that emit the most GHGs and the second largest polluter of freshwater globally, representing no less than 20% of total water consumption in the world[147].

If the fashion industry keeps this rhythm, pumping about 1.7 billion tons of CO_2 per year into the atmosphere, by 2050, the sector alone will be responsible for the consumption of a quarter of the world's carbon budget[148].

From the perspective of its social impact, the vast majority of the 80 billion pieces purchased each year in the fashion industry are produced in low- or middle-income countries where labor environment is particularly very poorly

---

[147] ELLEN MAC ARTHUR FOUNDATION, *A new textiles economy: Redesigning fashion's future*, 2017. Available at: http://www.ellenmacarthurfoundation.org/publications.

[148] UNITED NATIONS ENVIRONMENTAL PROGRAMME. Putting the brakes on fast fashion. https://www.unep.org/news-and-stories/story/putting-brakes-fast-fashion, 2018.

in terms of safety conditions and wages, contributing to reduced costs and keep the prices of the garments very cheap[149].

For instance, most manufacturers workers in Bangladesh are women who are paid the equivalent of 0.27 euros cents per hour in shifts of more than 12 hours per day, which is still insufficient to cover their basic needs[150].

Over the past 15 years, consumers have purchased an average of 60% more clothing than they need. In the same period, the production and consumption of garments has doubled at a rapid pace, and the average utilization that corresponds to the number of times an item of clothing was worn significantly decreased (36% between 2000 and 2015)[151].

According to the UN Environment Program, every second, the equivalent of a garbage truck of textiles is

---

[149] One example of the possible negative consequences of these precarious labor conditions occurred on 24 April 2013 with the Rana Plaza disaster in Dhaka, Bangladesh. Functioning as a host textile workshop for five garment factories and plenty of workers exposed to unsafe conditions, this building, composed of 8 floors, 3 of which were constructed illegally, collapsed, killing at least 1,132 people and injuring more than 2,500. Just five months earlier, also in Dhaka, there was another tragic disaster involving the garment sector in Bangladesh, where at least 112 workers lost their lives. These tragedies, which rank among the worst industrial accidents on record, awakened the global community to the poor working conditions faced by textile workers in Bangladesh.
[150] BICK, R., HALSEY, E., & EKENGA, C. C. *The Global Environmental Injustice of Fast Fashion. Environmental Health, 17*(1). https://doi.org/10.1186/s12940-018-0433-7, 2018.
[151] ELLEN MACARTHUR FOUNDATION. *Circular Business Models: Rethinking business models for a thriving fashion industry*. Available at: https://www.ellenmacarthurfoundation.org/fashion-business-models/overview, 2021.

landfilled or burned. About three-fifths of all garments are estimated to end up in incinerators or landfills within one year of production. Textiles are estimated to account for approximately 9% of annual microplastic losses to the ocean[152].

Fast fashion exemplifies the obsolescence strategy at this sector. It is characterized by low-cost but stylish clothing that flows rapidly from design to retail stores to attend to market trends, with new collections being introduced incessantly.

By compressing production cycles and creating updated designs, these companies allowed shoppers to expand their wardrobes and quickly update them. In almost every clothing category, consumers keep clothing items about half what they did 15 years ago. Some estimates suggest consumers treat lower-priced garments as nearly disposable, discarding them after seven or eight uses[153].

Whitehead Lorh clarifies the situation, arguing that once upon a time, there were two fashion seasons: Spring/Summer and Fall/Winter. Fast forward to 2014, and the fashion industry is churning 52 "micro-seasons" annually.

---

[152] On a global scale, textile waste represents nearly 92 million tons per year, 12% downcycled and only 1% recycled. Therefore, 73% of this waste is incinerated or in landfills, causing pollution and loss of habitat and biodiversity (GRANSKOG, A. et al. *Biodiversity: The next frontier in sustainable fashion*, McKinsey & Company, 2020).

[153] REMY, N. et al. *Style that's sustainable: A new fast-fashion formula*. Available at: https://www.mckinsey.com/capabilities/sustainability/our-insights/style-thats-sustainable-a-new-fast-fashion-formula, 2020.

With new trends coming out every week, the goal of fast fashion is for consumers to buy as many garments as possible as quickly as possible[154].

The largest retailer in the world, Zara Inditex is the pioneer of fast fashion with a highly responsive supply chain that ensures total control over its activities with incredible speed and flexibility.

The data collected from the retail stores feed the company's product development to guarantee a continuous renewal of new trendy and customer-driven products[155].

The manufacturing process lasts around three weeks, and the stores reload twice a week to avoid the cumulation of unsold products and still meet demand. With this great variety from one delivery to another, the consumer has the impression of buying a unique piece that only some have had the opportunity to purchase[156].

---

[154] WHITEHEAD LOTH, S. *5 Truths the fast fashion industry doesn't want you to know*. Huffington Post. https://www.huffpost.com/entry/5-truths-the-fast-fashion_b_5690575, 2014.

[155] AFTAB et al., 2018. *Super Responsive Supply Chain: The Case of Spanish Fast Fashion Retailer Inditex-Zara*. International Journal of Business and Management; Vol. 13, No. 5. https://www.iberglobal.com/files/2018/zara_case_supply_chain.pdf; 2018.

[156] HANSEN, S. *How Zara Grew Into the World's Largest Fashion Retailer*. The New York Times. https://www.nytimes.com/2012/11/11/magazine/how-zara-grew-into-the-worlds-largest-fashion-retailer.html, 2012.

The business strategy adopted by Zara Inditex in fast fashion stimulates the consumer's desire to make instant purchases and not wait for the sale period.[157].

Another big retailer in the fast fashion industry is H&M, which in 2022 faced accusations of "*greenwashing*"[158], meaning they were making false or misleading claims about their sustainability efforts, mainly through the use (or misuse) of the Higg Index, which is H&M's sustainability certification system.

The Higg Index is a tool designed to assess a product's environmental impact throughout its lifecycle, from design to disposal. However, H&M's self-reported Higg Index scores were often inaccurate or inflated, and the company was not fully transparent about its environmental impact.

In response to the accusations of greenwashing, H&M has made a strong commitment. The company has pledged to intensify its efforts and become fully transparent

---

[157] JIN, B., CHANG, H. J. J., MATTHEWS, D. R., & GUPTA, M. Fast Fashion Business Model. *Fashion Supply Chain Management*, 193–211. https://doi.org/10.4018/978-1-60960-756-2.ch011, 1982.

[158] According to Hayes, greenwashing is a deceptive practice where organizations make false, misleading, or untrue claims about their company, product, or service's positive impact on the environment. In other words, it refers to elaborating unsubstantiated claims to deceive consumers into believing that a company's products are environmentally friendly or have a more significant positive environmental impact than they do (HAYES, A. *What Is Greenwashing? How It Works, Examples, and Statistics*. Available at: https://www.investopedia.com/greenwashing, 2024).

about its environmental impact. This includes publishing a list of suppliers and disclosing the environmental impact of each product and other relevant data. Additionally, the company has set ambitious sustainability goals, as outlined in H&M's latest sustainability report.

These goals include using 100% sustainably sourced materials by 2030 and reducing absolute greenhouse gas (GHG) emissions across the value chain by 56% by 2030 and at least 90% by 2040. The remaining 10% of unavoidable emissions will be removed through carbon dioxide removals to reach net zero by 2040[159].

The strategies implemented by H&M following the greenwashing scandal represent a proactive new phase in the company's sustainability efforts to change its reputation as a fast fashion company. According to these new claims, the

---

[159] The Climate Dictionary of the UNDP defines *carbon removal* as the process of eliminating greenhouse gas emissions from the atmosphere. This can be done through natural solutions such as reforestation and soil management, as well as technological solutions like direct air capture and enhanced mineralization. While carbon removal is not a replacement for reducing greenhouse gas emissions, it can help slow down climate change and is necessary to shorten any period during which we temporarily exceed our climate targets. On the other hand, carbon capture and storage (CCS) is a distinct process that involves capturing carbon emissions produced by fossil fuel power plants or other industrial processes and storing them deep underground to prevent them from entering the atmosphere. CCS could be effectively used to address emissions from sectors that are difficult to decarbonize, such as heavy industries like cement, steel, and chemicals. (UNITED NATIONS DEVELOPMENT PROGRAMME. *The Climate Dictionary: Speak Climate Fluently*, p. 11. New York: UNDP, 2023).

company aims to not only achieve a net-zero carbon footprint by removing greenhouse gases from the atmosphere, but also reduce its impact on water resources, help protect biodiversity, and support human rights such as health, livelihoods, land rights, and access to water[160].

4.3. Sustainable Consumption and Circularity

As noted earlier, planned obsolescence is very present in the foundations of the linear economy paradigm. It is an integral part of production and consumption processes through the conscious acceleration of the valuable life cycle of goods and services and their consequent purchase.

Of course, as hyper-consumption and planned obsolescence underpin the linear economy, they hold back the rise of a circular economy system[161]. This situation leads us to rethink the idea of consumption within a circular mindset and associate it with sustainability as proposed by the emblematic Brundtland Report: *"Perceived needs are*

---

[160] H&M. *Sustainability: Circularity and Climate.* Available at: https://hmgroup.com/sustainability/circularity-and-climate/.

[161] Rachel Botsman and Roo Rogers explained the quest faced by sustainable consumption in simple words: *"Our challenge is not the fundamental consumer principle in itself but the blurred line between necessity and convenience; the intoxicating addiction of defining so much of our lives through ownership, and the never-ending list of things we "have to have". And hyper-consumption has brought us to a place where the real cost of bargain is that some consumers will trample over a man in the quest for a good deal"* (What's mine is Yours: The Rise of Collaborative Consumption").

socially and culturally determined, and sustainable development requires the promotion of values that encourage consumption standards that are within the bounds of the ecologically possible and to which all can reasonably aspire"[162].

According to this concept, and as confirmed in the first part of this chapter, culture and social background influence the values, ideas, and behaviors reflected in interactive practices such as consumption.

Vergragt stated that a sustainable lifestyle reduces ecological impacts while enhancing prosperity. Adopting a sustainable life to satisfy our needs and wants is conditioned, facilitated, and constrained by societal norms, political institutions, public policies, infrastructures, markets, and culture[163].

Of course, within a system that stimulates hyper-consumption and planned obsolescence, it is necessary to gather different stakeholders to reverse this situation and include consumption patterns inside the planetary boundaries in a socially balanced and fair way to ensure that the

---

[162] United Nations, *Report of the World Commission on Environment and Development: Our Common Future*, 1987.
[163] VERGRAGT, P.J. et al. *Fostering and Communicating Sustainable Lifestyles: Principles and Emerging Practices*, UNEP– Sustainable Lifestyles, Cities and Industry Branch, http://www.oneearthweb.org/communicating-sustainable-lifestyles-report.html, 2016.

products and services we consume are designed not to harm our environment but to increase sustainably our living standards.

From the perspective of the private sector, companies need to reconsider their business models to use natural resources more efficiently. This involves considering the entire life cycle of a product, from manufacturing to disposal and encouraging consumers to make conscious choices that reduce waste and promote sustainability[164].

One illustration of efforts from the public authorities to enhance sustainable consumption is the *"Resolution on Longer Lifetime for Products: Benefits for Consumers and Companies,"* approved by the European Parliament in July 2017. This resolution aims to tackle planned obsolescence, providing incentives for companies that produce durable and high-quality goods and encouraging and facilitating the reparability of products for consumers[165].

---

[164] This idea aims to reduce end-user consumption using strategies such as durability, warranties, and reparability to build products that last and circulate for a long time, participating incessantly in the supply chain. However, to break and consolidate paradigms through an innovative business model that aims to rethink ownership and offer a leased model through long-term relationships to promote shared value for people and the planet according to efficiency, sufficiency, and equity principles.

[165] By taking measures to ensure consumers to access durable, high-quality products that can be repaired and upgraded, the European Union wants to promote a longer product lifespan, in particular by tackling programmed obsolescence, according to the follow recommendations: *a)* robust, easily repairable ,and good quality products: "minimum resistance criteria" to be established for each product category from the design stage; *b)* if a repair takes longer than a month, the guarantee should be

Another example is the introduction of the Digital Product Passport (DPP) in the EU market with the approval of the Eco-design for Sustainable Products Regulation in 2024[166]. This mechanism provides consumers with clear information about the life cycle of the products they are purchasing and plays a crucial role in promoting sustainable product choices by indicating whether they comply with environmental standards.

Consumers can track a product's life cycle by scanning a unique digital code, which provides information such as technical performance, materials, and their sources, repairability, recycling capabilities, and environmental footprint.

This approach enables consumers to make informed, sustainable decisions by providing access to product details

---

extended to match the repair time; c) member states should give incentives to produce durable and repairable products, boosting repairs and second-hand sales - this could help to create jobs and reduce waste; d) consumers should have the option of going to an independent repairer: technical, safety or software solutions which prevent repairs from being performed, other than by approved firms or bodies, should be discouraged; e) essential components, such as batteries and LEDs, should not be fixed into products, unless for safety reasons; f) spare parts which are indispensable for the proper and safe functioning of the goods should be made available "at a price commensurate with the nature and life-time of the product"; and g) an EU-wide definition of "planned obsolescence" and a system that could test and detect the "built-in obsolescence" should be introduced, as well as "appropriate dissuasive measures for producers".

[166] Chapter 3 also discusses the Eco-design for Sustainable Products Regulations (ESPR) and the Digital Product Passport (DPP), illustrating the application of the principle of efficiency in a circular economy.

and helping them determine if the product aligns with their expectations. It improves the clarity, accessibility, and reliability of product information regarding circularity and sustainability for all stakeholders.

By making more sustainable choices, consumers can contribute to the conservation of natural resources, reduce the amount of waste in landfills, and protect the planet for future generations. When consumers choose products without considering their environmental impact, they create significant waste that can take years to break down.

The option for products composed of eco-friendly materials, for example, made from recycled material or produced using renewable energy or even locally sourced products to reduce transportation-related emissions, contributes to the practice of sustainable consumption.

In conclusion, sustainable consumption involves broader societal implications, engaging different stakeholders and their choices, from consumer behavior by choosing, for instance, products with minimal packaging to business strategies by reducing waste and pollution and governmental policies by promoting consumer education and awareness.

Therefore, sustainable consumption comprises a practice that aims to guide consumer behavior towards environmentally friendly, socially equitable, and economically viable use of products and services to minimize our impact on the planet and to ensure the responsible and efficient management of natural resources.

Transparency and raising awareness are critical factors in stimulating sustainable consumption practices at different levels of our society.

Transparency is crucial for ensuring sustainable consumption. It promotes accountability and encourages responsible behavior by providing consumers with clear information about their purchases, the materials used, and where those materials go when they are reintroduced into the value chain.

The adoption of sustainability standards is an essential governance instrument for enhancing transparency[167], serving as a roadmap to facilitate the transition to a green economy and to guide the integration of circular practices into business operations, instilling a sense of accountability[168].

---

[167] The uses of certified sustainability standards, such as organic or fair-trade labels, are categorized as non-state, market-driven governance approaches that aim to improve the economic, environmental, and social sustainability of production. These standards empower businesses to produce goods and services under sustainable, environmental, and social conditions. The United Nations Forum on Sustainability Standards (UNFSS), conceptualize them as *"specifying requirements that producers, traders, manufacturers, retailers or service providers may be asked to meet, relating to a wide range of sustainability metrics, including respect for basic human rights, worker health and safety, the environmental impacts of production, community relations, land use planning and others"* (UNFSS. *1st Flagship Report of the United Nations Forum on Sustainability Standards (UNFSS)*. Available at: https://unfss. org/home/flagship-publication/, 2013).

[168] MARX, A and WOUTERS, J. *Is everybody on board? Voluntary*

Since consumers and other stakeholders cannot observe or experience the production conditions directly, sustainability standards act as a bridge, illuminating the gap with transparency and trust and thereby ensuring that the production conditions align with the consumers' perceived values[169].

Typically, sustainability standards are accompanied by a verification process known as certification. This process evaluates whether an enterprise complies with a standard and provides a traceability process for certified products. This traceability assures consumers of the product's sustainability and enhances their preference for such products.

One example of the circular certified standard is the Cradle to Cradle, which is based on the idea that each raw material used in one product should be reusable, not losing any value along the supply chain.

The companies are evaluated according to five categories of sustainable performance to obtain the *Cradle to*

---

sustainability standards and green restructuring. Development (Basingstoke). https://doi.org/10.1057/s41301-016-0051-z, 2015.

[169] The sustainability standards require performance in areas such as management effectiveness, branding, product quality, attributes, production and processing methods, and sustainable supply chains. They are not just about individual businesses. They emphasize capacity building and collaboration, working with partners and other organizations to support smallholders or disadvantaged producers in making the social and environmental improvements needed to meet the standard. This collaborative approach makes the audience feel part of a more significant, impactful movement.

Cradle certification: material health, product circularity, clean air, climate protection, water and soil stewardship, and social fairness[170].

Hence, transparency requires access to track and understand the supply chain of the products and services used to establish consumer trust. Consequently, companies are progressively adopting innovative solutions such as blockchain technology to enhance transparency.

By implementing blockchain for tracking materials and products across the supply chain, recording every transaction, and enabling traceability back to its origin, companies are staying ahead of the curve and keeping consumers well-informed.

Another critical factor in promoting circular consumption practices is raising awareness, which relies on providing comprehensive education about the importance of consumer choices and the negative impact of unsustainable consumption patterns. This can be accomplished through various measures, including formal educational programs in schools and universities, informal community initiatives, and public campaigns to engage citizens[171].

---

[170] CRADLE TO CRADLE PRODUCTS INNOVATION INSTITUTE. *Cradle to Cradle Certified.* Available at: https://c2ccertified.org/the-standard.

[171] The Circular Economy Alliance emphasizes that circular thinking is relevant not only to industries but also to education, which serves as the foundation for its propagation. Educational institutions are crucial in

Advocating with policymakers and other key stakeholders is a potent force for change. This can involve lobbying to reform regulations, promoting sustainable practices in business operations and supply chains, and empowering consumers to make a difference.

Another way to contribute is through various forms of media, such as films, documentaries, news articles, and social media posts, which can potentially educate people and galvanize public support for sustainable consumption practices.

Disseminating the sustainability case across different sectors of our society through educational programs and giving consumers information and the necessary tools to know where their products and services come from can revert our current consumption patterns.

---

preparing a new generation that is equipped, motivated, and dedicated to leading our world toward a circular and sustainable future. This is achieved through the following initiatives: 1. Establishing Foundational Knowledge: Providing basic concepts of circularity. 2. Encouraging Critical Thinking: Developing analytical skills based on real-world challenges. 3. Promoting Interdisciplinary Learning: Offering a holistic perspective and covering the complexity and interdependencies of circularity. 4. Cultivating Responsible Citizenship: Capacity building for conscientious consumers. 5. Facilitating Research & Innovation: Driving technological and methodological advancements. 6. Building Collaborative Networks: Implementing partnerships that can lead to community-based projects, seminars, and workshops to disseminate circular thinking (CIRCULAR ECONOMY ALLIANCE. *The Role of Education in Promoting Circular Thinking.* Available at: https://circulareconomyalliance.com/cea-blogs/the-role-of-education-in-promoting-circular-thinking/, 2023).

Businesses and consumers must be part of this strategy, and public authorities must contribute to setting the course towards more sustainable consumption patterns tackling planned obsolescence.

4.3.1. Circular Fashion Industry

Applying the strategies of eliminating waste by keeping resources in use at a high rate, the approach proposed by the circular fashion aims to design and produce garments to be reused, recycled, or upcycled rather than discarded after a couple of uses. This new mindset is gaining much attention and popularity as consumers become more aware of the environmental and social impacts of the fashion industry[172].

In the circular fashion, clothes are produced from sustainable materials such as organic cotton and other eco-friendly fabric, designed for longevity and durability and to be recycled or upcycled at the end of their life cycle, aiming at reducing environmental impacts (such as carbon footprint

---

[172] The Ellen Mac Arthur Foundation proposed four ambitions goals to orient the textile economy towards circularity: 1. Phase out substances of concern and microfibre release; 2. Transform the way clothes are designed, sold, and used to break free from their increasingly disposable nature; 3. Radically improve recycling by transforming clothing design, collection, and reprocessing; and 4. Make effective use of resources and move to renewable inputs.

and waste) while maximizing value by keeping products and materials in use at a high rate.

There is also the social impact of the transition towards a circular fashion business model that offers the opportunity to review the value distribution more equitably across the textile supply chain and improve stakeholder collaboration and transparency.

Brent et all highlight that circular fashion can provide strong job creation that is more multifunctional, stimulating positions, and with better security. More entrepreneurial opportunities and a significant potential to integrate informal workers while offering social protection[173].

The outdoor clothing Brand Patagonia is an essential case of a company that has embraced circular fashion in its business model. The company has integrated multiple initiatives to reduce waste and promote circularity, including a program that stimulates customers to repair their worn or damaged clothes to extend their garments' life cycle[174].

---

[173] BRENT, M. et al. *Keeping Workers in the Loop: Preparing for a Just, Fair, and Inclusive Transition to Circular Fashion*. BSR. Available at: https://www.bsr.org/en/reports/circular-fashion-keeping-workers-in-the-loop, 2021.

[174] In 2017, Patagonia launched a product life extension program called Worn Wear in response to the fact that 85% of clothing ends up in landfills or gets incinerated. The program aims to keep its gears in use longer and reduce overall consumption. Through this trade-in and resale model, consumers can return Patagonia gears in decent condition in exchange for store credit. These returned items are then resold on Patagonia's online platform. To date, Worn Wear has successfully sold over 120,000 repurposed Patagonia items (PATAGONIA. *Worn Wear.*

Patagonia also uses sustainable materials to generate a closed-loop recycling system for its polyester products. The company acknowledges that the biggest challenge to its environmental footprint comes from materials manufacturing, which accounts for about 85% of its emissions every year.

One of the ways Patagonia practices environmental responsibility is by using only organically grown cotton in all products made from virgin cotton since 1996. They are also working to increase the use of preferred materials, such as organic and Regenerative Organic cotton, hemp, recycled polyester, and recycled nylon[175].

The measures taken by Patagonia against hyper-consumerism are well illustrated through its brand activism[176] in the campaign "*Don't Buy This Jacket*", a full-page

---

Available at: https://wornwear.patagonia.com)
[175] Patagonia's commitment to sustainability starts with a careful preffered material selection process. According to their data, the percentage of preferred materials across all fabrics has increased from 43% in 2016 to 88% in 2022 and is projected to reach 91% in 2024. By Fall 2024, 99% of their styles will incorporate some amount of preferred material (PATAGONIA. *Our Environmental Responsibility Programs.* Available at: https://www.patagonia.com/our-responsibility-programs.html).
[176] In Chapter 3, we explored the concept of brand activism within the framework of SDG 12, Target 12.8 (please refer to pages 104-105). For instance, Patagonia demonstrates brand activism through its self-imposed Earth tax: 1% for the Planet initiative. The company contributes a percentage of its earnings to environmental non-profit organizations that defend our air, land, and water around the globe, emphasizing its commitment to promoting public awareness about conserving and restoring natural ecosystems.

advertisement published in the New York Times on Black Friday in 2011.

DON'T BUY THIS JACKET

The idea of the "*Don't Buy This Jacket*" campaign was to raise consumers' awareness about Patagonia's products' environmental impact and encourage them to buy less and repair and reuse their Patagonia clothing.

On its website, Patagonia explained the reasons behind the campaign: *"It would be hypocritical for us to work for environmental change without encouraging customers to think before they buy. To reduce environmental damage, we all have to reduce consumption as well as make products in more environmentally sensitive, less harmful ways. It's not hypocrisy for us to address the need to reduce consumption. On the other hand, it's folly to assume that a*

150

healthy economy can be based on buying and selling more and more things people don't need—and it's time for people who believe that's folly to say so"[177].

This innovative campaign emphasizes the relevance of consumer awareness about the impact of their purchases and how companies can contribute to promoting social and environmental change. Patagonia's sales increased after the campaign launched, demonstrating how a company can be profitable and sustainable.

Another interesting example is the Dutch jeans brand MUD, founded in 2012, which aims to transform the fashion industry by implementing an innovative circular business model.

Aware that producing one pair of jeans requires 7.000 liters of water and different chemical components, MUD implemented an innovative model based on recycled cotton and washing techniques that uses 393 liters of water, saving 6.607 liters of water compared to an industry standard.

Moreover, using this method combined with low-energy techniques and land and water transportation, one pair of MUD Jeans emits 75% less CO_2 than the industry standard.

---

[177] PATAGONIA, *Don't Buy This Jacket, Black Friday and the New York Times*. Available at: https://www.patagonia.com/stories/dont-buy-this-jacket-black-friday-and-the-new-york-times/story-18615, 2011.

To minimize the consumption of virgin material to save water and energy, protect biodiversity, and reach those numbers, MUD decided to base a significant part of its production on discarded cotton, achieving an average of 40% of its jeans made from post-consumer recycled cotton. To collect these raw materials, the company allows consumers to return worn jeans from its brands and any others if they are composed of 98% cotton.

To reduce its environmental footprint and promote social impact, the other 60% of the cotton used by MUD Jeans comes from long-lasting relations built with selected vital partners that produce organic cotton and are committed to sustainable practices certified by Global Organic Standard (GOTS), which means work in fair and safe conditions, and that no pesticides, insecticides, or toxic chemicals are used[178].

MUD Jeans are designed to be recycled, as they are very basic and composed of practically only one material (their buttons are made of 100% stainless steel that can also be easily recycled).

According to the numbers provided by the company, MUD Jeans has already ensured that 20,000 jeans have not ended up in landfills, 1.5 million kilos of CO_2 have been

---

[178] To be part of MUD's supply chain, these partners signed its Code of Conduct based on fair wages for workers, a safe and healthy labor environment, and equality regardless of race, gender, age, shape, or ability.

avoided, 550 million liters of water have been saved, and 160 m2 of land has been preserved[179].

By rethinking the idea of ownership in its business model, the company also provides the possibility to buy and lease jeans for 9,95 euros per month for 12 months, after which the customer can choose to keep them or exchange them for new lease jeans. It is important to emphasize that this leasing model contributes to the accessibility of sustainable fashion to a larger group of consumers, as it is more affordable than purchasing a new one that costs around 119,95 to 149,95 euros.

Currently, MUD Jeans is considered an exemplary circular fashion company, one of the world's first B Corps, pioneering the *"Lease a Jeans"* model in 2013 and putting the circular economy principles into practice.

The transition to circular fashion involves implementing innovative business models aimed at reducing the environmental impact of design by using durable fibers and eco-friendly techniques. It also involves promoting efficient production methods to conserve raw materials and optimize energy consumption.

Furthermore, as an ethical alternative to fast fashion, circular business models should create systems to ensure transparency. This will help to showcase their impact and

---

[179] MUD Jeans. Available at: https://mudjeans.nl, 2022.

illustrate their connections across the supply chain with partners who share similar values rooted in higher labor and environmental standards[180].

Finally, it promotes a circular lifestyle by encouraging consumers to buy clothes made from sustainable materials, opt for second-hand clothing, repair and upcycle their existing clothes, consider the environmental impact of their choices, and be willing to make a change.

4.3.2. Collaborative Consumption

The concept of collaborative consumption, also known as the sharing economy, is still in its early stages. There are several terms used to describe this phenomenon, including peer economy, crowd economy, access economy, and gig economy. All these terms revolve around the idea of replacing traditional ownership with digital or physical platforms that connect people and allow them to share access to goods or services.

---

[180] To reduce the environmental and social impact of the fashion industry, promoting its transition towards circularity will require joint efforts across multiple actors involved in this sector, as in the case of the Zero Discharge of Hazardous Chemicals, a coalition formed by 22 apparel brands to improve and expand the use of nontoxic, sustainable chemistry in the textile and footwear supply chain; or the Better Cotton Initiative composed by more than 50 retailers and brands and nearly 700 suppliers in defining standards for environmental, social, and economic responsibility in cotton production.

According to Rachel Botsman and Roo Rogers, collaborative consumption is an economic model based on sharing, swapping, trading, or renting products and services, enabling access over the ownership. It is reinventing not just what we consume but how we consume[181].

Driven by network technologies, especially the internet and mobile devices, this system facilitates direct transactions that connect people in unprecedented ways. It enables individuals to share assets they own, such as a hammer, house, or party tent, thereby transforming the traditional relationship between producer and consumer[182].

A collaborative economy differs from traditional forms of exchange in terms of the number and type of actors involved. Tucci and Laskowski explain that it consists of three parties: the platform, an owner, and a seeker. The platform creates a virtual space where users (owner and seeker) can exchange and monetize underused belongings[183]. According to the principles of collaborative consumption, its business model can be characterized as a triadic relationship rather than a dyadic one.

---

[181] BOTSMAN, R. and ROGERS, R. *What is mine is yours: The Rise of Collaborative Consumption*. Harper Collins Publishers, 2010.
[182] MOATTI, S. C. *The Sharing Economy's New Middlemen. Harvard Business Review*. Available at: https://hbr.org/2015/03/the-sharing-economys-new-middlemen, 2015.
[183] TUCCI, L. & LASKOWSKI, N. *Definition: Sharing Economy*. Available at: https://www.techtarget.com/searchcio/definition/sharing-economy, 2018.

From the perspective of circularity, collaborative consumption unlocks the idling capacity of all kinds of assets, reducing pressure on natural resources and providing consumers with more efficient ways to meet their needs.

Huang and Rust explain that participation in collaborative consumption helps reduce overconsumption by allowing individuals to acquire, use, and dispose of their assets in a way that positively influences environmental, economic, and social sustainability by changing the consumption cycle[184].

Through innovative business models, particularly digital platforms, underutilized resources can be reinserted into the value chain, preventing them from ending up in landfills and making them available for exchange as goods or services again, to connect individuals and businesses in a global movement of collaborative consumption.

In this context, the collaborative economy is characterized by the efficient use of resources and a reduced need to purchase more physical goods. As a result, there is an impact on physical production, which minimizes the consumption of natural resources and reduces negative impacts on the environment, such as the emissions of greenhouse gases and chemical pollutants[185].

---

[184] HUANG, M. H., RUST, R. T. *Sustainability and Consumption.* Journal of the Academy of Marketing Science 39 (1), 40–54, 2011.
[185] Mi and Coffman provided an example of the transportation sector to

Founded in 2015, the Danish platform Too Good to Go (TGTG) is an example of an innovative circular platform that aims to tackle food waste by connecting its customers to excess food from nearby restaurants and supermarkets that would otherwise be discarded, as explained by the company: "*Food waste is a big problem, and we can be a solution. Too Good Too Go is the app that lets you rescue unsold food at your favourite spots from an untimely fate*"[186].

The app allows customers to buy "*Magic Bags*" of prepared foods, fresh produce, and baked goods at a discount retail price and pick them up in-store at a predetermined time, typically 30 minutes before closing.

---

illustrate the relationship between collaborative economy and environment through vehicle-sharing behavior that "*can have a positive environmental impact by decreasing the number of kilometers travelled. Such sharing activities can also stimulate long-lived changes in consumer behaviour by shifting personal transportation choices from ownership to demand-fulfilment. Similarly, bicycle sharing schemes can reduce the use of motorised vehicles that usually consume petroleum products and generate emissions. In Shanghai, bicycle sharing reduced carbon dioxide (CO_2) and nitrogen oxide (NO_X) emissions by 25,000 tonnes and 64 tonnes in 2016, respectively*" (MI, Z., COFFMAN, D. *The Sharing Economy promotes Sustainable Societies. Nat Commun* 10, 1214: https://doi.org/10.1038/s41467-019-09260-4, 2019).

[186] Onyeaka and Chukwugozie support our points about Too Good to Go's circular approach. They emphasize that the company helps reduce food waste by ensuring that surplus food is consumed rather than wasted. Additionally, it raises awareness about food waste and promotes responsible consumption among consumers (ONYEAKA, H. and CHUKWUGOZIE, D. C. *Closing the Loop: How Circular Economy Approaches Can Tackle Food Waste and Promote Sustainability*. SUSTAINE.ORG, Vol. 1, n. 1. Available at: https://sustaine.org/journal/index.php/sciences/article/view/11, 2023).

The company generates revenue by charging its partners a fixed order-based fee and a yearly administrative fee. Currently, TGTG has over 50 million users in 17 countries worldwide and has helped prevent the waste of over 100 million meals.

The company's business model is based on the triple bottom line approach, as indicated on its website, where it explains the reasons for addressing food waste: "*Economic - wasting food costs us $1.2 trillion each year; Environmental - food waste is responsible for 10% of greenhouse gas emissions (that's more than the whole aviation industry); and Social - we waste 2.5 billion tonnes of food annually, whilst 828 million people go hungry every day*"[187].

In the fashion industry, collaborative consumption is crucial for promoting sustainable consumption patterns by exchanging secondhand clothes and other underutilized garments. Vinted, a platform for pre-owned pieces founded in 2008 in Lithuania, exemplifies this concept and has become one of the largest online retailers for secondhand fashion in Europe.

Users can buy and sell various items on Vinted through a user-friendly interface for listing and searching.

---

[187] TOO GOOD TO GO. Available at: https://www.toogoodtogo.com/en-ca, 2023.

This provides a convenient way to exchange unwanted items and empowers users to earn extra money[188].

Vinted's mission is to promote sustainable fashion by encouraging people to buy and sell secondhand clothing instead of purchasing new items. Their slogan, "*Don't wear it? Sell it!*" emphasizes the goal of prolonging existing apparel's lifespan and reducing textile waste. The platform has gained popularity by raising awareness about the environmental impact of fashion[189].

In conclusion, considering the growing interest in these platforms, it is relevant to better understand this phenomenon by identifying its benefits and challenges. The

---

[188] Domingues, Zambrano, and Rodriguez explain that Vinted relies on the choices made by its users. It targets a consumer profile that chooses to complete the product's useful life instead of consuming and discarding it insatiably. For these consumers, Vinted broadens the traditional means to reuse (chain of sharing with family, acquaintances, and charities) and offers them a way to increase savings, generate income, and be environmentally respectful. By giving products a second life, Vinted synthesizes its commitment to sustainable consumption and significantly reduces the environmental impact of fast fashion, making its users feel more environmentally conscious and responsible (DOMINGUEZ, I. P., ZAMBRANO, R. E. and RODRIGUEZ, V. A. *Gen Z's Motivations towards Sustainable Fashion and Eco-Friendly Brand Attributes: The Case of Vinted*. MDPI Sustainability 15(11), Available at: https://www.mdpi.com/2071-1050/15/11/8753#B21-sustainability-15-08753, 2023).

[189] Based on information from its website, Vinted is a prominent platform for buying and selling second-hand clothing and other items. It has over 65 million users and employs more than 1200 people. The platform operates in 16 countries: Austria, Belgium, Canada, France, Germany, Italy, Lithuania, Luxembourg, Poland, Portugal, Slovakia, Spain, the Netherlands, the Czech Republic, the UK, and the USA (VINTED. *About us*. Available at: https://www.vinted.com/about).

benefits of a Collaborative Economy include increasing efficiency by facilitating the everyday use of resources, reducing costs by changing ownership to collective access to goods and services, fostering innovation by generating new opportunities for entrepreneurs and businesses, and improving social cohesion by connecting people and sharing resources. Simultaneously, the challenges that must be addressed to develop the collaborative economy include regulatory aspects and the need for more comprehensive research to enhance trust and confidence.

5. INNOVATION AND CIRCULAR ECONOMY

5.1. The Concept of Innovation

Today, '*innovation*' has become a buzzword, representing multiple things. Understanding these multiple meanings is crucial, as it allows us to use the term appropriately and preserve its core meaning. Therefore, it is relevant to contextualize the purpose of its use to discover the proper concept of what 'innovation' is, especially within the domains of the circular economy and its agents.

Etymologically, the term innovation originates from the Latin verb "*innovare*", which means to renew, to do something new to promote a specific change in something established, especially by introducing new methods, ideas, or products[190]. Such a word symbolizes a change related to successful ideas that create a new way of doing something.

With its transformative power, innovation explores the creative human spirit to translate ideas into something new and plays a significant role in shaping human behaviors.

By recognizing opportunities and generating value, innovation influences how we interact with our environment and adapt to the changes around us.

---

[190] OXFORD ADVANCE AMERICAN DICTIONARY. Available at: https://www.oxfordlearnersdictionaries.com/definition/american_english/innovation.

At the core of any innovative process, there is Creativity, which Parkhurst defines as *"the ability or quality displayed when solving unsolved problems, when developing novel solutions to problems others have solved differently, or when developing original and novel (at least to the originator) products"*[191].

Thus, creativity represents the act of thinking of something new that results in new and valuable ideas. It is the catalyst that allows us to intervene in the real world and bring about change.

On the other hand, innovation refers to converting these ideas into something tangible. Mintzberg conceptualizes innovation as a way to break away from established patterns and do things differently[192]. It is an unlimited renewable resource supported by knowledge that changes and adds value to a given system.

Following this relation, Bolton and Thompson consider creativity the starting point, whether it is associated

---

[191] PARKHURST, H. B. *Confusion, lack of consensus, and the definition of creativity as a construct. Journal of Creative Behavior, 33*(1), 1-21, 1999. Creativity is the foundation of innovation, as Amabile et al. referred to it as the "seed" of innovation (AMABILE, T. M. et al., *Assessing the Work Environment for Creativity.* Academy of Management Journal, 39, 1996) or McLean, who observed that without creative ideas, innovation is an engine without fuel (MCLEAN, L. D. *Organizational Culture's Influence on Creativity, and Innovation. A Review of the Literature and Implications for Human Resource Development.* Advances in Developing Human Resources, 7, 2, 2005).
[192] MINTZBERG, H. *Structures in Fives: Designing Effective Organizations.* London: Prentice Hall, 1983.

with invention or opportunity spotting. This creativity is turned into a practical reality through innovation.

However, this transformation is not always straightforward. It can be hindered by various factors such as lack of resources, resistance to change, or even fear of failure. Innovation, which is settled in the context of an enterprise to add new value, often requires overcoming these challenges.[193].

Innovation exploits "*change*" driven by constant adaptation and transformation of a given system to foster growth. It involves a strategic factor that can be disciplined, cultivated, learned, applied, and practiced, and the outcome (change) is understood as an opportunity to add value to the system to be transformed[194].

In other words, innovation is not a random process; it is a systematic effort that requires a combination of energy, vision, passion, commitment, judgment, and risk.

It is about recognizing opportunities, finding resources, developing initiatives, and capturing the resulting value. This emphasizes the need to be proactive and forward-thinking in the innovation process.

---

[193] BOLTON, B. and THOMPSON, J. *Entrepreneurs, Talent, Temperament, Technique.* Butterworth Heinemann, Oxford, 2000.
[194] DRUCKER, P. *Innovation and Entrepreneurship: Practices and Principles.* Harper & Row, New York, 1985.

5.1.1. Creative Destruction

Indeed, the pioneering and inspiring ideas of the Austrian economist Joseph Schumpeter, elaborated in the early 20th century, are highly significant for a better understanding of the characteristics and dynamics of innovation. By relating it to the concept of entrepreneurship, Schumpeter's ideas explained how these elements have historically played a relevant role in generating wealth and economic growth.

According to Schumpeter, the starting point for the analysis of innovation is based on the circumstance that capitalism is unstable. It represents an evolutionary process; its fundamental problems originated from this fact.

Second, this evolution does not result from the effects of external factors as "*prime movers*" such as population growth, shocks, wars, or natural disasters, among others, but in a kind of economic mutation that is caused by innovation. This innovation is not a random occurrence, but a deliberate act carried out by entrepreneurs, who play a pivotal role in Schumpeter's theory[195].

Schumpeter understood capitalism as an evolutionary process that constantly pursues new markets and

---

[195] SCHUMPETER, p. 76, 1967. For Schumpeter, entrepreneurs are the engine of economic growth and prosperity, as they are seen as responsible for productive activity, that is, for experimenting with new "combinations of materials and forces".

opportunities. In this context, innovation is a survival strategy for enterprises. It is the key to sustaining long-term economic growth and adapting to the ever-changing market dynamics.

As Schumpeter defines it, innovation involves the creation of new products, services, and production processes, the exploration of new markets and resources, and the search for more efficient forms of organization.

In this order of considerations, Schumpeter emphasized that innovation differs from invention[196] as it configures an instrument situated in the economic system to meet commercial purposes through combinations of new or existing factors, such as knowledge and resources, to introduce market novelties and capture its respective

---

[196] In the entrepreneurial context, the distinction between innovation and invention is crucial. Invention involves the creation and implementation of new ideas, while innovation is the process of extracting financial value from these ideas. This distinction is significant as it highlights the economic potential of innovation. One historical example is Thomas Edison, who was unsuccessful at introducing his inventions to the marketplace. As a result, his sponsors had to remove him from every new business he founded. This illustrates the importance of successful implementation, not only in scale but also in meeting customer needs. Therefore, successful innovations generate economic profits as a reward for introducing the invention into the market. It is also relevant to highlight Schumpeter's idea of diffusion, which plays a crucial role in spreading innovation. This concept represents the communication of innovation among the members of society through specific channels, enlightening us about how new ideas are spread and their adopters identified.

economic benefits. This innovative process would generate at least one of the following outcomes:

a) elaboration of a new good;

b) adoption of a new method of production;

c) creation of a new market;

d) establishment of a new source of supply of raw material; and

e) application of a new organization of any industry (or market)[197].

By enabling new combinations of factors and promoting technological changes, innovation provides a strategic advantage that leads to profits, monopolistic practices, the creation of new companies, and a complete reorganization of the market[198]. The emergence of identical products or other innovations helps to balance competitive relationships until the cycles are repeated with the inevitable change of the "*rules of the game*".

The process of such mutation is known as "*Creative Destruction*" which was introduced in his 1942 book:

---

[197] SCHUMPETER, J. A. *The Theory of Economic Development: An Inquiry into Profits, Capital, Credit, Interest and the Business Cycle*, New Brunswick (U.S.A) and London (U.K.): Transaction Publishers, 1934..

[198] DÁVILA, A. O. *Economia de la innovación y del cambio tecnológico: una aproximación teórica desde el pensamiento Schumpeteriano*. Revista Ciencias Estratégicas. Vol 16 - No 20, p. 244, 2008.

"*Capitalism, Socialism, and Democracy*". This term is characterized by the ongoing destruction of the "*old*", the dismantling of outdated business and economic models, and the pursuit of creating the "*new*" through revolutionary technologies and innovative methods to improve living standards.

The process of mutation revolutionizes the entire economic structure. It continuously destroys the old structure and creates a new one, disrupting long-standing practices and procedures. This disruption clearly signals the necessity of change to keep up with market trends, liberating resources and energy for innovation.

The destructive element was necessary as a form of manifestation of the entrepreneurial spirit that sets and keeps the capitalist machine in motion by offering the opportunity to seek profit. It not only reaps the rewards of innovation for its front-runners but also penalizes those who do not follow the trends towards progress, growth, and better living standards[199].

Considering its impact on the economic system, creative destruction changes the entire nature of markets. It drives out traditional businesses that do not adapt their models to the dominant innovative factors, as pointed out by

---

[199] SCHUMPETER, J. A. *Capitalism, Socialism and Democracy*, p, 120. HarperCollins, 1968 (2008).

Schumpeter: *"Situations emerge in the process of creative destruction in which many firms may have to perish that nevertheless would be able to live on vigorously and usefully if they could weather a particular storm"*[200].

Of course, this idea is directly related to the competitive market forces. According to Schumpeter's framework, these forces are balanced under long waves of innovation, where business cycles operate[201].

Schumpeter observed that each of these cycles is unique and driven by different clusters of industries. The development of a cycle began with the introduction of a new set of innovations:

- Water power, textiles, and iron in the late 18th century

- Steam, rail, and steel in the mid-19th century

- Electricity, chemicals, and the internal combustion engine in the early 20th century[202].

---

[200] SCHUMPETER, J. A. *Capitalism, Socialism and Democracy*. Harper Collins, 1968 (2008).

[201] For Schumpeter, a healthy economy is constantly disrupted by technological innovation, leading to 50-year cycles of economic activity, as the Russian economist Nikolai Kondratieff observed earlier. In 1925, Kondratieff observed long waves of economic activity by analyzing data on prices, wages, and interest rates in France, Britain, and the USA. However, about 10 years later, Stalin executed him due to his accurate prediction that Russian farm collectivization would lead to a decline in farm production. This political event had significant implications for economic research, as it led Schumpeter to take on the task of studying these waves (BURNS, P. *Entrepreneurship and Small Business: Start-up, Growth and Maturity*, p. 31. London: Palgrave, 2016).

[202] These booms eventually declined as the technologies matured and the market opportunities were fully exploited, only to begin again with a new

Consider the profound impact of the railway industry, which redefined urban demographics and trade at the turn of the 19th century. More recently, the internet has emerged as a powerful force of creative destruction, dismantling established business practices and paving the way for market novelties, including innovative technologies, products, and new forms of production and distribution.

It is important to understand that competitive markets are not static; they are dynamic and constantly changing. This dynamic nature requires businesses to innovate and adapt continuously. Those who succeed in this effort thrive, while those who fail to do so are inevitably left behind.

There are winners and losers in this open-ended Darwinian game of creative destruction. However, it is not only about the survival of the fittest; it is about resilience. The ability to adapt and bounce back can significantly increase the chances of a business not just surviving, but thriving, in the new economic order.

The process of creative destruction does not always mean the immediate elimination of all businesses in a particular sector. Instead, it involves a gradual and qualitative replacement of these businesses.

---

set of innovations that changed how things were done. Schumpeter observed the cyclical nature of economic activity, which reassures the predictability of these patterns (SCHUMPETER, J. A. *Capitalism, Socialism and Democracy*. Harper Collins, 1968).

Once more, the railway's impact on transportation can help us visualize our previous considerations, as it did not completely eliminate the need for horse-drawn transportation. In fact, it actually increased the demand for horses for short-distance transport[203].

Furthermore, it is essential to note that the rise of the internet did not imply the extinction of all non-digital businesses. Instead, they continue to coexist, deprived of the competitive advantage incorporated by those who have explored the innovation provided by the virtual world and its opportunities.

To characterize innovation as a competitive advantage means comprehending it as a temporary factor that attributes value creation to goods or services until the competitors can duplicate them or a new cycle of creative destruction, a process where new innovations replace older ones, comes around.

In this ever-evolving landscape, developing specific strategies to overcome the destructive side of innovation cycles is a necessity and a testament to businesses' adaptability. These strategies allow them to create models that can foresee the unexpected, withstand competitive threats, and seize opportunities.

---

[203] ANDERSEN, E. S. *Evolutionary economics post-Schumpeterian contributions*. Pinter, Lond, 1994.

5.1.1.2. Circularity and Creative Destruction

Schumpeter's theory of innovation was developed to address the economic context of the last century. In the 21st century, new complexities influence the conception and dynamics of essential concepts in his theory, such as capitalism, innovation, entrepreneurship, and creative destruction.

Based on previous verification, the pursuit of change and its symptoms present opportunities and form the progressive nature of capitalism and the sources of innovation. Therefore, it is essential to reassess Schumpeter's theory by recognizing the challenges of a globalized society and guiding innovation toward addressing its current needs.

Today, a growing need to promote social inclusion and protect the environment is leading capitalism in a new direction. This direction is not just about profit maximization and market conquest but also about creating a positive impact on people and the planet. It's about fostering new patterns of relationships based on solidarity and cooperation.

The central question is how to use innovative solutions to benefit society and the environment. This requires a fundamental reshaping of the roles of different actors, promoting new relationships and collaborative models. It's a collective effort emphasizing the importance of working together toward common goals.

In today's world, the concept of creative destruction needs to guide capitalism towards circularity. This shift not only inspires entrepreneurs but also has the potential to generate wealth in a way that aligns with this new mindset. In this context, circular innovation emerges as a disruptive agenda that can transform the operation of various systems in a global society.

With the intensification of globalization, there has been a significant increase in interdependence and connectivity among people and cultures. This has dramatically impacted entrepreneurs' strategic decisions to drive disruptive innovation and address common global issues.

In essence, the widespread occurrence of common global problems highlights the pressing need for creative solutions that can positively benefit society and the environment. This need calls for a reevaluation of the roles of various stakeholders, including nation-states and businesses, to cultivate new forms of partnerships and change the current logic of value creation.

Considering this scenario, innovation involves creating more excellent economic and social value while using fewer resources. It means pursuing the symptoms of change and proposing creative solutions to meet societal needs guided by a circular mindset, which aims to convert adversity into opportunity and do more with less.

Frugal Innovation exemplifies the previous idea; it refers to a process of creating simple, affordable, and sustainable products and services accessible to a mass audience formed by low-income groups.

This approach aims to tackle global challenges by providing accessible and innovative solutions that are cost-effective and have a significant social impact on customers in developing countries, especially for those at the bottom of the pyramid.

Prahalad and Hart argue that in a globalized society, inclusive capitalism should focus on addressing the needs of two-thirds of the world's population, many of whom live near or below the poverty line with an average income of less than $2 per day. Providing these people with basic needs such as food, water, shelter, and healthcare requires high levels of creativity[204]. They also suggest that beyond addressing

---

[204] PRAHALAD, C. K. and HART *The Fortune at the Bottom of the Pyramid.* Berkeley: Strategy+Business, issue 26. Available at: https://people.eecs.berkeley.edu/~brewer/ict4b/Fortune-BoP.pdf, 2002. The progress of shared value in this context involves reevaluating conventional market rules and challenging fundamental assumptions. They describe this as a managerial challenge for the world's wealthiest companies: selling to the poor and helping them improve their lives by producing and distributing products and services in culturally sensitive, environmentally sustainable, and economically profitable ways.

poverty, there is a significant opportunity for innovative technology and business models to make a positive impact, generating shared value by rethinking products and markets[205].

According to Navi Radjou and Jaideep Prabhu, frugal innovation converts limited resources into an opportunity to use human creativity to extract value from unimagined places, according to the following principles:

1. *"Keep it simple"*, do not create solutions to impress consumers (easy to use, widely accessible).
2. *"Do not reinvent the wheel"*, leverage existing resources and assets widely available.
3. *"Think and act horizontally"*, scale-out horizontally through your supply chain[206].

Frugal Innovation is crucial for successful entrepreneurship in the 21st century. It involves converting the most abundant resources into inputs to address what is scarce. It's not about doing more for more, as traditional business models suggest in their linear system. Instead, it's about doing more with less (*sufficiency*), doing it better (*efficiency*), and making it accessible (*equity*). This approach saves resources and leads to better, more accessible solutions.

---

[205] Chapter 2 introduces the concept of shared value, based on Porter and Kramer, as a new logic of value creation aligned with circularity and the triple bottom line (see pp. 56-59).
[206] RADJOU, N. and PRABHU, J. *Frugal Innovation: How to Do Better with Less*. Economist Book, 2015.

5.2. Circular Innovation and Business Strategies

Circularity refers to the renovation of how we generate wealth, produce goods and services, structure our societies, and value the nature of our planet. The transition from linear to circular economy demands the transformation of practically all business structures and procedures, which is where circular business strategies come into play and create wealth based on shared value and triple-bottom-line approaches[207].

---

[207] Better World Books, a company based in the US, exemplifies a business model built upon the idea of creating value through shared value and triple-bottom-line approaches. Better World Books was founded in 2002 by University of Notre Dame students. They received seed money from the university's social venture plan competition. The company is a for-profit social enterprise that sells both used and new books online. Better World Books has adopted the triple bottom line as a core value of its business model. This means they believe profits are not the only way to measure business success. They aim to balance social, economic, and environmental values for all their stakeholders, demonstrating their alignment with the idea of shared value. The company collects and sells books online to save millions of used books from landfills while creating jobs and supporting educational and literacy programs and libraries. Better World Books has over eight million new and used titles in its stock and has raised over $28 million for literacy initiatives worldwide. Following the slogan "doing well by doing good," when a customer purchases a book from Better World Books, one book is donated to people in need through non-profit organizations partnered with the company, such as Books for Africa and Feed the Children. It is also possible to track this donation system through the Impact Map on the company's website. (SMITH, G. *Better World Books: A Case Study in Sustainability*. https://www.gregoryasmith.info/research/better-world-books, 2020).

In other words, circularity is about how our economic systems are changing. This change necessitates the adoption of new business mindsets and models that are focused on resource efficiency, sufficiency, and equity. These new approaches open new opportunities for innovation and guide society toward sustainable production and consumption patterns.

E. Guldmann sustained that *"circular business models are special in the sense that they look for value creation in places usually of little interest to companies that operate in the traditional linear production paradigm"*[208]. Businesses can accelerate the shift toward circularity by designing and implementing their activities to balance profits with social and environmental impacts.

For example, the implementation of closed-loop business models involves creating systems where products are designed to be reused or recycled at the end of their lifecycle. These models not only promote the use of eco-friendly designs and green value chains but also tackle the current status quo on hyper-consumption.

In this circular strategy, the producers are responsible to manage the end-to-end material flows, and the burden of waste is not concentrated only on the customers. This

---

[208] GULDMANN, E. *Best Practice Examples of Circular Business Models*, 2014.

approach involves engaging the entire supply chain to enhance resource efficiency, prolong the product's life cycle, and repeatedly recapture its value at a high rate[209].

5.2.1. Business Values and Circular Strategies

From a business perspective, creating value by implementing a circular mindset in a company involves rethinking the existing value proposition offered to customers and the entire supply chain[210] and how it can encompass four value-creation processes:

- *Sourcing Values*
- *Environmental Values*
- *Customer Values*
- *Information Values*

The sourcing values are closely tied to profitability and encompass all the direct cost reductions and savings that arise from implementing closed-loop supply chains. In

---

[209] Resource efficiency aims to extend product value, creating multiple relationships among stakeholders: manufacturers, consumers, and their peers to use waste as a resource intentionally; it means collecting and obtaining "wasted" materials or resources to transform them into new forms of value. This strategy aims to convert waste into goods and services, creating synergies where products are recollected, reconditioned, and reintroduced into a new value chain. Of course, applying resource efficiency as a business strategy is closely linked to the principle of efficiency described in Chapter 3 (see p. 66-68).

[210] GEISSDOERFER, M., MORIOKA, S. N., DE CARVALHO, M. M., & Evans, S. *Business models and supply chains for the circular economy*. Journal of Cleaner Production, 190, 712–721, 2018.

essence, they pertain to the direct financial benefits that can be derived from adopting closed-loop business practices.

For example, refurbishing products and adopting recycled materials cannot only open new market opportunities, but also generate more revenues. In the long run, the company can also reduce operational costs by developing the capacity to reuse materials.

Circular value chains can enhance the capacity to reuse existing materials, reducing dependency on volatile resources affected by fluctuating prices or availability. As a result, they contribute to financial gains, savings, and improved management of resource supply and cycles, leading to more resilient and sustainable business models.

Once companies integrate the sourcing values into their business models, they can improve their ecological footprint by implementing a closed-loop system. In terms of environmental value, meaningful communication is essential. Without effective communication that engages stakeholders, there is no tangible business value in contributing to environmental and biodiversity protection.

From the perspective of environmental value, increasing footprints brings two key benefits: ease of compliance and an improved green image. When companies communicate their positive environmental actions, they can attract new customers and enhance the loyalty of existing ones. Equally important, they can also play a proactive role in informing governmental institutions, such as environmental protection agencies or regulatory bodies, about their actions, thereby contributing to the planning and development of operations in accordance with environmental regulations.

Customer value refers to increased loyalty, improved satisfaction, and enhanced superior brand protection. Aligning the business model with the closed-loop supply chain involves providing a new range of products and services when customers return a product, such as offering a discount on their next purchase or exchanging their product for a new one.

Companies can also have the opportunity to create a catalog featuring environmentally friendly or refurbished products to expand customer options and increase satisfaction and loyalty, demonstrating the effectiveness of this business strategy in generating value through a customer-centric approach.

A recent study developed by IBM and the National Retail Federation verifies the relevance of circularity in increasing customer loyalty. The study discovered that 57% of US consumers agree to change their purchasing behaviors to contribute to mitigating environmental impact.

Once companies have implemented reverse logistics and taken back their products, they can inspect them to access valuable data on production and supply chain processes. This allows them to learn about their customers' preferences regarding how they are using or not using the products as expected.

Thus, this data can significantly improve various supply chain processes and product design, leading to substantial financial benefits. This eliminates the need for expensive third-party sources, providing a more cost-effective way to access this valuable information.

For example, companies in the fashion industry can increase their sourcing values by capitalizing on revenue streams focused on circular models, including redistribution, remanufacturing, repairs, resale, and recycling of worn-out products. These practices contribute to reducing their ecological and social impacts, capture additional economic value by offering a new line of sustainable products, build customer loyalty to the brand, and provide relevant data. This data, when used effectively, can provide valuable insights to enhance the overall business operation.

Furthermore, these companies become more resilient as they can reduce costs by using low-priced materials through secondary utilization and avoiding expensive product disposal.[211].

5.2.2. Data for Circularity

One innovative approach to identifying and implementing circular goals involves leveraging data to shape comprehensive strategic decision-making and action plans[212].

---

[211] SCHÖNBERG, H. *Creating value with data in circular business models of textiles*. Available at: https://aaltodoc.aalto.fi/items/6ae10fee-bcc8-42cd-ac41-12bea33ffb89, 2022.

[212] The relevance of using data for social outcomes is highlighted in the World Development Report 2021, which adopts the theme "*Data for Better Lives*". This report explores the significant potential of the evolving data landscape to improve the lives of impoverished individuals while also recognizing its risks, which can negatively impact individuals, businesses, and entire societies. A key focus of the report is the concept of Data for Development (D4D). It underscores the importance of using data more strategically and effectively to achieve various developmental outcomes. This requires a well-functioning governance framework that ensures infrastructure, laws, economic policies, and institutions work together to support data usage that aligns with societal values while safeguarding individuals' rights regarding their data. This framework should establish the rules and compliance mechanisms for all stakeholders to share, use, and reuse data safely. Using data effectively helps governments and organizations create better public policies that meet community needs. A data-driven approach improves program design, ensuring initiatives to address the specific challenges faced by marginalized groups. It also emphasizes the importance of delivering services efficiently. Data helps track and evaluate how well these services work, allowing for continuous improvements in quality and accessibility. Furthermore, the report shows that using data wisely can improve market efficiency. Businesses can make informed decisions that promote growth and create jobs by analyzing data trends. Overall, integrating data into these processes can drive economic development and improve people's lives in vulnerable communities (WORLD BANK. *World Development Report 2021: Data for Better Lives*. Washington: International Bank for Reconstruction and Development/The World Bank. Available at: https://www.worldbank.org/en/wdr2021).

Firstly, to effectively discuss data for circularity, it is essential to contextualize it within the broader framework of Big Data[213]. Big Data involves the management and analysis of large quantities of information obtained from various sources, including social media, sensors, transactions, and more. This data is processed quickly to generate valuable insights for an organization.

Therefore, by harnessing advanced technologies such as machine learning and artificial intelligence, businesses can adopt data modeling and forecasting techniques to conduct in-depth analyses of their existing processes and assess their alignment with circular objectives.

Data for Circularity encompasses a comprehensive analysis of the hidden patterns in human experiences and the exchange of ideas to uncover previously unknown correlations that contribute to formulating effective circular business strategies[214]. These strategies aim to enhance

---

[213] At the core of the Big Data framework are the five Vs, which define its characteristics: 1. *Volume* refers to the enormous amounts of data generated every second; 2. *Velocity*: data is generated at an unprecedented speed, necessitating rapid processing to extract actionable insights in real time; 3. *Variety*: data comes in multiple formats, including structured (like databases) and unstructured data (like text, images, and videos), which requires sophisticated tools and techniques for practical analysis; 4. *Veracity*: it deals with the accuracy and credibility of the data for making informed decisions; 5. *Value*: the primary objective of utilizing data is to create significant value, and organizations must focus on translating it into insights that can be applied as business strategies (SAGIROGLU, S. *Big data: A Review*. 2013 International Conference on Collaboration Technologies and Systems (CTS). pp. 42–47, 2013)

[214] Data analysis is a valuable technique for modeling material flows and

resource efficiency and facilitate closing the loop within the supply chain[215].

The effective use of data can drive innovation in product, service, and business models, ultimately transforming how businesses operate.

For example, companies can analyze large datasets to assess energy consumption patterns, resource utilization, and waste generation. This data-driven approach can uncover inefficiencies and pinpoint areas for improvement[216].

Moreover, predictive analytics can forecast the potential impacts of changes[217], enabling businesses to make

---

complex systems and assessing the environmental impact on business operations. Companies can uncover hidden correlations, patterns, and causal relationships within data sets related to circularity metrics, stakeholder interaction, and supply chain dynamics by employing advanced analytics methods- such as predictive modeling, machine learning, and algorithms. (DUBEY, R. et al. *Examining the role of big data and predictive analytics on collaborative performance in context to sustainable consumption and production behaviour.* Journal of cleaner production n. 196, 1508-1521, 2018).

[215] CHEN, D., PRESTON, D. and SWINK, M. *How the Use of Big Data Analytics Affects Value Creation in Supply Chain Management.* Journal of Management Information Systems 32(4): 4–39, 2015.

[216] GROVER, V., CHIANG, R., LIANG, T. and ZHANG, D. *Creating Strategic Business Value from Big Data Analytics: A Research Framework.* Journal of Management Information Systems 35(2): 388–423, 2018.

[217] There are four primary types of analytics, each playing a critical role in supporting and informing various data-driven business decisions that enhance their performance and competitive edge. These types include: 1. Descriptive Analytics involves easily read and interpreted data to create reports and visualize information. It helps to analyze past performance and optimize company performance and operations. 2. Diagnostic Analytics seeks to explain the reasons behind a problem. It involves in-depth data analysis to dissect issues and understand the factors behind

informed decisions that support their circular initiatives and fully leverage data by altering their business model[218].

The transformative potential of data analytics in circular business models brings with it a variety of significant challenges.

A significant challenge in data management is the pressing need for standardized protocols. These frameworks ensure consistency and reliability across different data sources, enabling accurate analysis and reporting.

Establishing comprehensive structures that integrate all levels and relevant components related to data-driven decision-making is imperative. Such frameworks would simplify the complexities of integrating and analyzing data effectively[219].

Additionally, managing a complex supply chain is significantly dependent on both the quality and availability of

---

business outcomes to prevent similar problems in the future. 3. Predictive Analytics examines past and present data to forecast trends, customer needs, and market dynamics, ultimately guiding strategic planning using statistical models and machine learning techniques. 4. Prescriptive Analytics recommends actions based on predictive outcomes using algorithms and optimization techniques to evaluate various scenarios and suggests the best course of action to maximize results or minimize risks (COTE, C. *Insights: 4 Types of Data Analytics to Improve Decision-Making*. Harvard Business School Online. Available at: https://online.hbs.edu/blog/post/types-of-data-analysis, 2021).

[218] BUHL, H., RÖGLINGER, M., MOSER, F. and HEIDEMANN, J. *Big Data, Business & Information Systems Engineering* 5(2): 65–69, 2013.

[219] TEKINER, F. and KEANE, J. *Big Data Framework*. IEEE International Conference on Systems, Man, and Cybernetics, Available at: https://ieeexplore.ieee.org/document/6722011, 2013.

data. In these systems, data can often encounter various challenges, including incompleteness, where essential information is missing[220]; fragmentation, where data is scattered across multiple sources, making it difficult to access and analyze[221]; and obsolescence, where data becomes outdated and no longer reflects current realities[222].

---

[220] Incomplete data are questions without answers or variables without observations (GANTAYAT, S.S., MISRA, A., and PANDA, B.S. *A Study of Incomplete Data – A Review.* Advances in Intelligent Systems and Computing vol. 247, Switzerland: Springer International Publishing, 2013). It often comes from missing information at critical points in the supply chain. This can happen for several reasons, such as delays in sharing information between suppliers and manufacturers, mistakes in tracking inventory, or poor communication among departments. Additionally, external factors like sudden changes in demand or logistical problems can make it harder to keep accurate records. In conclusion, not having complete data can cause serious problems with the analysis, leading to wrong decisions and imperfect knowledge that impact overall operational efficiency.

[221] Data fragmentation resides in disparate systems that are not integrated affecting to information about products, materials, and processes, which is frequently dispersed across multiple platforms. As a result, it becomes difficult to achieve a comprehensive understanding of the performance of the circular economy. This fragmentation can limit insights into how resources are utilized and recycled, thereby impeding the ability to optimize operations. Addressing data fragmentation is crucial for enabling better decision-making and fostering a more efficient approach to resource management (WANG, L. and ALEXANDER, C. A. *Big Data Driven Supply Chain Management and Business Administration.* American Journal of Economics and Business Administration, 7 (2): 60-67, 2015).

[222] Data extraction, transformation, and decision-making delays can result in value loss. Using outdated information can distort our view of current operations, resulting in poor decisions (PIGNI, F. *Digital Data Streams: Creating Value from the Real-Time Flow of Big Data*, California Management Review 58: 5–25, 2016). Relying on inaccurate information can result in incorrect conclusions, particularly in supply chains, where recent trends and disruptions may be overlooked. Outdated information complicates the integration of various data sources, creating

These issues can lead to inefficiencies, poor decision-making, and ultimately hinder the overall performance of the supply chain. Ensuring high-quality, accessible, and up-to-date data is thus crucial for optimizing operations and achieving strategic circular objectives[223].

Furthermore, barriers to stakeholder collaboration can significantly impact the success of data-driven circular models. Due to differing interests, goals, and commitment levels, organizations often struggle to engage diverse stakeholders, such as suppliers, customers, and regulatory bodies[224].

Collecting and sharing data collaboratively is essential for realizing the value of data in a networked circular economy to maintain an efficient flow of information along the supply chain and implement innovative solutions[225].

---

inconsistencies and gaps that harm analysis accuracy. This inefficiency needs to be revised to ensure decision-making reliability, making it challenging to meet market demands, allocate resources effectively, and identify areas for improvement.

[223] WANG, L. et al. IoT-Enabled Real-time Energy Efficiency Optimization Method for Energy-Intensive Manufacturing Enterprises. *International Journal of Computer Integrated Manufacturing*, *31*(4-5), 362-379, 2018.

[224] GUPTA, S., CHEN, H., HAZEN, B., KAUR, S. and SANTIBAÑEZ GONZALEZ, E. *Circular economy and big data analytics: A stakeholder perspective, Technological Forecasting and Social Change*, 2018.

[225] BROWN, P. *Why do Companies pursue Collaborative Circular oriented Innovation?* Sustainability (Switzerland) 11(3), 2019.

Lastly, organizations often need enhanced analytical capabilities to leverage the fully potential of data analytics. Even when managed responsibly, effectively utilizing data typically demands significant investments in management, technology, and other resources[226].

Many businesses need more tools and expertise to conduct in-depth analyses or to translate data into actionable strategies. Consequently, they may overlook opportunities to enhance their circular goals and overall efficiency.

In conclusion, a comprehensive approach is essential for effectively addressing data-driven challenges related to circular objectives.

This involves implementing robust data integration strategies that unify several sources, actively engaging stakeholders to promote collaboration and mutual understanding, and developing personalized analytical tools tailored to the challenges of circularity within the digital ecosystem.

These efforts aim to improve asset utilization, enhance operational efficiency, extend customer experiences, and ensure information transparency[227].

---

[226] AKTER, S., WAMBA, S. F., GUNASEKARAN, A., DUBEY, R. and CHILDE, S. J. *How to improve firm performance using big data analytics capability and business strategy alignment?* International Journal of Production Economics 182: 113–131, 2016.

[227] GÜNTHER, W., REZAZADE MEHRIZI, M., HUYSMAN, M. and FELDBERG, F. *Debating Big data: A Literature Review on realizing*

Organizations can integrate data-driven insights into their strategic planning by overcoming challenges and transforming data into actionable information and knowledge.

This approach helps guide decision-making and effectively reduces their environmental footprint while enhancing operational efficiency. Ultimately, it contributes to sustainability and promotes innovation and long-term resilience in business operations, allowing companies to thrive in a circular transition.

5.3. Circular Strategies and the Entrepreneurial State

The Entrepreneurial State promotes opportunities throughout the innovation chain by making visionary and strategic public investments. It aims to become a partner of the private sector and stimulate its *animal spirit*[228]. In this

---

Value from Big Data, The Journal of Strategic Information Systems, 2017.

[228] The concept of *'animal spirit'* is crucial in understanding how human emotions can significantly influence financial decision-making, especially in uncertain and volatile times. It describes the psychological and emotional factors that drive investors to take action when faced with high levels of volatility in the capital markets. When spirits are low, confidence levels will be low, which can lead to a decline in the market. Conversely, when spirits are high, confidence among participants in the economy will be high, increasing market prices. In their renowned book *"Animal Spirits: How Human Psychology Drives the Economy, and Why it Matters for Global Capitalism"*, published in 2009, Akerlof and Shiller argue that while animal spirits play a significant role, the government should equally intervene actively through economic policymaking when necessary. This intervention is crucial to control these animal spirits and

context, the State is willing to take risks and operate efficiently to generate growth opportunities and attract business investors.

Thus, the State acts as an entrepreneur by investing in areas where private capital hesitates to take risks. In this role, the State is not only a regulator but also an entrepreneur who promotes the most radical innovations that feed the evolution of capitalism[229].

Mariana Mazzucato argues that history shows us that innovation results from an extensive collective effort, not just the work of a small group of young white men in California. This means that the current global and historical impact of these ideas would only exist with a significant number of public investments behind the risk of uncertain technological ventures, such as the development of the computer and the Internet.

Overcoming the narrative that describes the State as "*boring and inertial*" means opening a path to wrap up successive waves of innovations and technologies to address pressing global challenges by implementing a circular agenda described by the SDGs.

---

prevent potential financial crises (TARDI, C. *Animal Spirits: Meaning, Definition in Finance, and Examples.* Investopedia. Available at: https://www.investopedia.com/terms/a/animal-spirits.asp, 2023).

[229] MAZZUCATO, M. *The Entrepreneurial State: Debunking public vs. private sector myths*, p 26. Penguin Books Ltd, 2014.

Therefore, we need a new mindset to characterize the role of the State as an entrepreneur in our society. This transformative shift can guide better public policies, assuming risks in research and investments that focus on creating and influencing markets rather than fixing their failures.

The concept of mission-oriented policies, which are systematic public policies that utilize cutting-edge knowledge to achieve specific objectives, is a powerful tool for change. Some describe it as *"big science deployed to meet big problems"*.[230]

Mariana Mazzucato emphasizes that through research and innovation, missions offer a focused approach to tackling the many challenges of today's society. This involves the participation of various stakeholders, each contributing to address critical questions: What are the key challenges facing society; how can concrete missions help solve those challenges; how can the missions be best designed to enable participation across different actors and empower them to engage in bottom-up experimentation, leading to system-wide innovation?[231]

---

[230] ERGAS, H. *'Does technology policy matter?'*, in Guile, B.R. and Brooks H. (eds.) Technology and global industry: Companies and nations in the world economy, Washington DC: National Academies Press, pp. 191-245, 1987.

[231] MAZZUCATO, M. *Mission-oriented research & innovation in the European Union: a problem-solving approach to fuel innovation-led*

In 2018, a report published by the European Commission[232] defined the criteria to characterize these missions. They should be ambitious, risky, and inspiring to citizens, with a clear target and deadline. According to these criteria, unambiguous answers are needed on whether the mission was completed by the deadline.

The missions should also be cross-disciplinary and cross-sectorial; for example, eradicating cancer requires health, nutrition, artificial intelligence, and pharmaceutical innovation.

Moreover, the missions should allow for experimentation and multiple attempts at a solution rather than being micromanaged top-down by a government[233].

The report mentioned what the missions might look like with a hypothetical example of a plastic-free ocean[234].

---

growth, European Commission, Directorate-General for Research and Innovation, Publications Office. Available at: https://data.europa.eu/doi/10.2777/360325, 2018.

[232] The plastic sector in the European Union is a significant part of its economy, employing 1.5 million people and generating a turnover of €340 billion in 2015. Europe produces a massive 26 million tons of plastic waste annually, but only less than 30% of this waste is collected for recycling. There is a huge potential for recycling plastic waste that could be turned into valuable resources to promote innovation, improve competitiveness, and create jobs. In January 2018, the EU adopted the European Strategy for Plastics as part of its circular action plan. The strategy is based on the concept of designing plastic products for recyclability. It represents a commitment to ensuring that all plastic packaging is cost-effectively reusable or recyclable by 2030, thereby significantly reducing the quantity of waste generated in this sector.

[233] MAZZUCATO, M. *The Value of Everything: Making and Taking in Global Economy*. Penguin Books, 2019.

The Clean Oceans mission could involve eliminating half of the plastic that already pollutes the oceans and reducing the amount of plastic entering the oceans by 90 percent by 2025. This will be achieved through initiatives like autonomous plastic collection stations and distributed networks. It also involves creating alternatives to plastic, designing innovative food packaging, and developing artificial intelligence systems for automated waste separation.

This innovative trans-sectorial approach, primarily through the partnership between public, private, and other developing actors towards circularity, presents a valuable opportunity to address wicked problems stemming from our existing production and consumption patterns.

---

[234] As versatile materials, plastics are used mainly in our society, offering several benefits to make our lives more convenient. However, they can also be a severe source of substantial problems, considering that their production depends on fossil fuels and their composting process can last for decades or centuries. A simple idea about the composting process of plastics can be illustrated through how they can remain in our ecosystems: plastic bags take 20 years, plastic bottles take 450 years, and coffee pods take 500 years. When the plastic renter as waste in the biosphere, it never really disappears, but it is converted into microplastics, endangering terrestrial and marine life by ingestion and absorption. Two relevant data help us understand the dimension of this wicked problem: 95% of the plastic consumed is discarded as waste after one single use, and by 2050, some estimations suggest that there will be more plastics than fish by weight in the oceans. Therefore, our relationship with plastic needs to be rethought, considering the current waste of using this material based on a take-make-waste linear model. The question that must be faced is how to close this loop, simultaneously retaining the value of plastics without seeping into our ecosystems.

It is particularly relevant in the context of the plastics system, where it can improve product design and resource efficiency while reducing its negative impact on the environment and society.

For instance, the Plastic Pact Network established by the Ellen MacArthur Foundation aims to connect national and regional circular solutions worldwide to enable knowledge sharing and coordinated actions, bringing together key stakeholders to confront plastic waste and pollution.

Each initiative is tailored to its geographic location and led by a local organization and unites businesses, government institutions, NGOs, and citizens supported by a shared vision with an ambitious set of local targets to:

- Eliminate unnecessary and problematic plastic packaging through redesign and innovation;
- Move from single-use to reuse;
- Ensure all plastic packaging is reusable, recyclable, or compostable
- Increase the reuse, collection, and recycling or composting of plastic packaging;
- Increase recycled content in plastic packaging[235].

---

[235] ELLEN MAC ARTHUR FOUNDATION. The Plastic Pact Network. Available at: https://ellenmacarthurfoundation.org/the-plastics-pact-network. To accelerate the transition to a circular economy for plastic through lessons learn and the effectively exchange of best practices across regions, the Ellen MacArthur Foundation's Plastic Pact Network

These proposals align with the concept of upstream innovation that aims to pursue the origins of a problem and its causes and deal with it from there through a holistic approach to address environmental and social issues at the source[236].

Instead of focusing on end-of-life solutions such as recycling or waste management, upstream innovation looks at the root causes of environmental and social problems. It tackles them there to prevent them from happening in the first place.

Upstream innovation can contribute to driving circularity by developing new technologies and processes that eliminate waste and reduce resource use. In the business

---

includes national plastic pacts in the UK, France, Chile, the Netherlands, South Africa, Portugal, the US, Poland, and Canada. Regional pacts include the European Plastics Pact and the Australia, New Zealand and Pacific Islands (ANZPAC) Plastics Pact.

[236] A non-profit organization in Kenya called Ocean Sole illustrates the holistic approach needed to implement circularity through upstream innovation. Ocean Sole empowers artisans in Kenya to create art from discarded flip-flops. The flip-flops are washed, upcycled, and transformed into artwork and functional products, which helps reduce waste and raise awareness of the pollution problem. It has a significant environmental impact. By using flip-flops instead of wood, Ocean Sole promotes recyclability and saves over five hundred trees annually. Ocean Sole's commitment to environmental conservation and social development goes beyond recycling. In a country with an unemployment rate of over 40%, Ocean Sole is making a significant difference in Kenyan low-income communities. It positively impacts over 1,000 Kenyans through flip-flop collection for recycling and direct employment. It contributes over 10-15% of its revenue to beach clean-ups, vocational and educational programs, and conservation efforts.

landscape, upstream innovation refers to enhancing the initial processes involved in creating or developing a product or service. This optimization improves the entire supply chain, leading to better quality, reduced costs, and increased efficiency.

For example, automotive companies are investing in developing new, more efficient battery technologies to enhance electric vehicle performance, which can reduce costs and promote wider adoption. Investing in innovative and sustainable agricultural techniques can enhance crop yields and improve the quality and quantity of food production in the food industry while minimizing environmental impact and reducing waste.

From an upstream innovation perspective, there is significant potential to design products and services with circularity in mind. This approach emphasizes the creation of items that can be easily repaired or upgraded, extending their lifespan and reducing waste, promoting business models that encourage the reuse and recycling of materials.

In conclusion, addressing plastic pollution is a collective responsibility that involves multiple stakeholders with a circular mindset. Innovative methods and processes play a vital role in this context, such as replacing single-use plastics with reusable alternatives like supermarket refilling stations. Equally important is the role of deposit return schemes in collecting plastics before they re-enter the biosphere as waste, a crucial step in tackling plastic pollution.

It is essential to prioritize the development of eco-friendly designs for plastic products by incorporating innovative solutions to minimize their impact on the environment.

One approach is utilizing sustainable polymers with recyclable, biodegradable, or compostable properties. Additionally, creating packaging that is entirely recyclable and crafted from bio-based raw materials effectively contributes to circularity[237].

---

[237] An example of an innovative business model contributing to tackling plastic pollution is Loop Industries' approach. It helps companies transform their packaging with sustainable solutions by selling and collecting reusable versions of single-use products. Its technology decomposes PET and polyester fibers into basic chemical components, creating high-purity PET for diverse applications, including food storage. This operation significantly reduces single-use plastics and packaging waste, conserves energy, and promotes resource efficiency. Loop's sustainable packaging solutions benefit the environment and reduce long-term production and waste disposal costs for brands, leading to improved profitability and growth. Their partnerships have reduced packaging costs by an average of 15% and contributed to increased revenues. In 2022, Loop reported a 25% growth in partner brand participation, indicating profitability and an upward trend in companies investing in sustainable packaging solutions (LOOP INDUSTRIES. *Mission and Vision*. Available at: https://www.loopindustries.com/en/about/mission-vision).

6. CONCLUSION

The evolution of our social and economic systems has resulted in a capitalist model that prioritizes the maximization of profits. This model is supported by a linear economy that operates on a "*take-make-dispose*" approach, where raw materials are extracted, processed, utilized, and then discarded after serving their initial purposes.

It is clear today that running a linear economic system indefinitely on a planet with finite resources has negative consequences, including the generation of waste and pollution that lead to global environmental stress. Consequently, these effects impact the availability and regeneration of living ecosystems, compromising their ability to meet the basic needs of present and future generations.

Therefore, we must change our production and consumption patterns to replicate an innovative cyclical model. This model emphasizes the interconnectedness of respecting nature, promoting social inclusion, and generating wealth. By prioritizing these elements, we can create an enduring environment where both people and the planet can not only survive but also thrive.

In this context, the 17 Sustainable Development Goals (SDGs) launched by the document *'Transforming Our World: The 2030 Agenda for Sustainable Development'* are a people-centered blueprint for global sustainability and human development. These goals and their targets, designed to guide global efforts, are comprehensive in nature, encompassing a wide range of objectives to create a more equitable, prosperous, and resilient society.

The SDGs are interconnected and emphasize that all aspects of the goals and targets are interdependent and must be addressed together to achieve a balance among the environmental, economic, and social dimensions of sustainable development.

At the core of this transformative agenda is the circular mindset, a comprehensive approach that rethinks how we generate wealth through the production of goods and services and how we structure our society to prioritize regenerative and distributive behaviors. This approach presents an opportunity to reshape our lifestyles, balancing economic prospects with environmental and social advantages.

While circularity is directly related to SDG 12 and its targets to promote sustainable production and consumption patterns, it is considered a toolbox for achieving a significant number of other SDGs that cut across various sectors that address our current major global challenges, including climate action, zero hunger, decent work and economic growth, and life on earth.

The circular mindset provides a unique framework for progress on sustainable development. It applies innovative methods to close the gap between production and consumption, unlock the capacity and value of all kinds of assets to meet human needs, and simultaneously minimize the pressure on the natural environment.

Based on the principles of efficiency, sufficiency, and equity, the circular mindset aims to prioritize societal values based on people and the planet rather than focusing solely on monetization or material possessions as a part of one's identity.

From this perspective, the current approach to creating value should not only revolve around maximizing profits through monetization but also prioritize environmental protection and social inclusiveness. The circular mindset promotes a sense of connection and empathy, where both nature and financial objectives are considered in the logic of value creation.

The Triple Bottom Line approach, combined with the concept of shared value, represents a new way of thinking about business success. It is not just about profits and shareholder value but also about considering the environmental and social impacts. This approach emphasizes businesses' strategies for rethinking products and markets, improving supply chain productivity, and giving back to the community and natural ecosystems where the company operates as part of the equation to shift waste into future resources.

Replicating our natural system where waste does not exist, the concept of "*Waste is Food*" in circularity emphasizes optimizing resource use and minimizing waste production. It involves using resources for as long as possible throughout the value chain, minimizing waste from the start, and recycling and reusing materials.

Designing out waste, keeping products and materials in use, and regenerating natural systems are innovative strategies to incorporate a circular mindset into our productive systems to develop eco-design products built to last, avoiding planned obsolescence and retaining their value for as long as possible.

Implementing this closed-loop system, where waste is reduced, and resources are conserved, reinforces respect for the limits of our planet on which the future development of humanity depends.

These strategies also aim to change our current consumption patterns, where consumers are encouraged to buy new goods and discard the old ones. This affects the lifespan of products, which is intentionally kept short to drive continuous purchasing by applying planned obsolescence in accordance with the principles of linear economics.

The circular mindset proposes a new way for humans to relate to things. It creates long-lasting and reusable products, rethinks ownership by offering a leasing model through long-term relationships and promotes shared value for both people and the planet based on the principles of efficiency, sufficiency, and equity.

Transitioning towards circularity requires collective impact, which involves key players from different sectors committing to a common agenda to solve specific social problems. It is essential to engage multiple stakeholders in following a roadmap and aligning our production and consumption patterns within the planetary boundaries in a socially balanced and fair manner. This means ensuring that the products and services we consume are designed to minimize environmental harm and improve our living standards sustainably.

From the business perspective, it is relevant to underscore that by adopting circularity through innovative approaches, companies can reduce production costs, enhance operational efficiency, develop environmentally sensitive products, and ensure corporate responsibility towards planetary boundaries.

Businesses have a considerable environmental, economic, and societal footprint at various levels. Their influence extends beyond their internal operations to encompass the complex network of relationships within their value chains. By engaging different stakeholders and actively contributing to fostering circularity, businesses can positively impact the lives of some of the most vulnerable individuals in society.

Public institutions should shift their mindset and start seeing themselves as entrepreneurs. The concept of an entrepreneurial state aims to encourage the active participation of public entities in the transition towards circularity. This can be achieved through strategic incentives and investments distributed across the innovation chain by engaging society in a visionary perspective that offers more opportunities for sustainable growth.

By leveraging combined resources and fostering innovative cross-sector collaboration, particularly through partnerships involving public, private, and other emerging entities, there is an opportunity to drive meaningful and impactful systemic change through the adoption of circularity aimed at addressing the challenges posed by our existing patterns of production and consumption.

Hence, it is crucial to have the full cooperation of all relevant parties to shift away from the linear economy model. Civil society, individuals, and communities all have a role to play. The transition to a circular economy will occur if we consider ourselves equals, without discrimination or distinctions. Humankind is one; we are all part of the same species living on this interconnected planet.

It is essential to understand that everything we produce to meet our needs relies on our natural systems. Therefore, prosperity is not something given. Instead, it depends on how we interact with the environment to extract goods and provide services we need to keep running the "*unlimited wants*" of our society. Collaboration, partnership, and cooperation are the driving forces that propel the engine of prosperity to transform the challenges of our social systems into opportunities for positive change.

We must foster global solidarity through a circular mindset, promoting cooperative actions in an interconnected and globalized world. Instead of persisting with an economic system that harms our environment and society and cannot address global systemic risks, we should focus on implementing global systemic changes based on circularity to address these risks effectively.

Ernani Contipelli is a Professor at Webster University - Campus Leiden and Tashkent, the United International Business Schools (UIBS), and the Central American Institute of Public Administration. He holds two post-doctorate degrees in Comparative Politics and a Ph.D. in Public Law. He has experience in the academic field in different countries and various publications on his research areas of interest: Sustainability, Circularity, and International Cooperation.

7. REFERENCES

AFTAB et al., 2018. *Super Responsive Supply Chain: The Case of Spanish Fast Fashion Retailer Inditex-Zara.* International Journal of Business and Management; Vol. 13, Available at: https://www.iberglobal.com/zara_supply_chain; 2018.

AKTER, S., WAMBA, S. F., GUNASEKARAN, A., DUBEY, R. and CHILDE, S. J. *How to improve firm performance using big data analytics capability and business strategy alignment?* International Journal of Production Economics 182: 113–131, 2016.

AMABILE, T. M. et al., *Assessing the Work Environment for Creativity.* Academy of Management Journal, 39, 1996.

ANDERSEN, E. S. *Evolutionary economics post-Schumpeterian contributions.* Pinter, Lond, 1994.

AMSTERDAM CIRCULAR STRATEGY 2020-2025. *The Amsterdam City Doughnut: A Tool for Transformative Action.* https://www.amsterdam.nl/en/policy/sustainability/circular-economy, 2020.

BAUMAN, Z. *Liquid Modernity.* Blackwell Publishing, 2006.

BAUMOL, W. J. and BLINDER, A. S. *Economics: Principles and Policy.* Thomson South-Western, 2003.

BERCKERMAN, W. *Sustainable Development: Is It a Useful Concept?* Environmental. Values 3: 191-209, 1994.

BESADA, H., POLONENKO, L. M. and AGARWAL, M. *Did the Millennium Development Goals Work? Meeting Future Challenges with Past Lessons.* Policy Press, 2017.

BEN & JERRY'S. *Ben & Jerry's Is Fighting for Climate Justice, One Scoop at a Time.* Available at: https://www.benjerry.com/whats-new/2021/10/ben-jerrys-fighting-for-climate-justice.

BENTON, D., HAZELL, J. and HILL, J. *The Guide to the Circular Economy: Capturing Value and Managing Material Risk*, Routledge, 2017.

BUHL, H., RÖGLINGER, M., MOSER, F. and HEIDEMANN, J. *Big Data, Business & Information Systems Engineering* 5(2): 65–69, 2013.

BICK, R., HALSEY, E., & EKENGA, C. *The Global Environmental Injustice of Fast Fashion. Environmental Health*, *17*(1). https://doi.org/10.1186/s12940-018-0433-7, 2018.

BIERMANN, F., KANIEB, N. and KIM, R. *Global governance by Goal-setting: the Novel Approach of the UN Sustainable Development Goals.* Current Opinion in Environmental Sustainability, 2017.

_____. *'Earth System Governance' as a Crosscutting Theme of Global Change Research.* Global Environmental Change. Human and Policy Dimensions, 326–337, 2007.

BISSCHOP, L., HENDLIN, Y. & JASPERS, J. *Designed to Break: Planned Obsolescence as Corporate Environmental Crime. Crime Law Soc Change* 78, 2022.

BOCKEN, N.M.P., DE PAUW, I., BAKKER, C., VAN DER GRINTEN, B. *Product design and business model strategies for a circular economy.* In: Journal of Industrial Production and Engineering 33(5): 308-320, 2016.

BOFFEY, D. *Amsterdam to embrace 'doughnut' model to mend post-coronavirus economy.* Available at: https://www.theguardian.com/world/2020/apr/08/amsterdam-doughnut-model-mend-post-coronavirus-economy, 2020.

BOLTON, B. and THOMPSON, J. *Entrepreneurs, Talent, Temperament, Technique.* Butterworth Heinemann, Oxford, 2000.

BOTSMAN, R and ROGERS, R. *What's Mine is Yours? The Rise of Collaborative Consumption.* HarperCollins, 2010.

BRIDGEWATER, P., KIM, R. and BOSSELMANN, K. *Ecological Integrity: A Relevant Concept for International Environmental Law in the Anthropocene?* Yearbook of international Environmental Law, Vol. 25, No. 1, 2015.

BRENT, M. et al. *Keeping Workers in the Loop: Preparing for a Just, Fair, and Inclusive Transition to Circular Fashion.* BSR. Available at:

https://www.bsr.org/en/reports/circular-fashion-keeping-workers-in-the-loop, 2021.

BROWN, C. *Buddhist Economics: An Enlightened Approach to the Dismal Science*. New York: Bloomsbury Press, 2017.

BROWN, P. *Why do Companies pursue Collaborative Circular oriented Innovation?* Sustainability (Switzerland) 11(3), 2019.

BURNS, P. *Entrepreneurship and Small Business: Start-up, Growth and Maturity*. London: Palgrave, 2016.

CASE, K. E. and FAIR, R. C. *Principle of Economics*. New Jersey: Pearson Prentice Hall, 2004.

CHEN, D., PRESTON, D. and SWINK, M. *How the Use of Big Data Analytics Affects Value Creation in Supply Chain Management*. Journal of Management Information Systems 32(4): 4–39, 2015.

CHESHIRE, D. *The Handbook to Building a Circular Economy*. RIBA Publishing, 2021.

CIRCLE ECONOMY. *Decent Work in the Circular Economy: An Overview of the Existing Evidence Base (joint report by Circle Economy, the International Labour Organization (ILO) and the Solutions for Youth Employment (S4YE) Programme of the World Bank)*. Available at: https://www.circle-economy.com/resources/decent-work-in-the-circular-economy.

CIRCULAR ECONOMY ALLIANCE. *The Role of Education in Promoting Circular Thinking*. Available at: https://circulareconomyalliance.com/cea-blogs/the-role-of-education-in-promoting-circular-thinking/, 2023.

COYLE, D. *The Economics of Enough: How to Run the Economy as If the Future Matters*. Princeton University Press, 2011.

COTE, C. *Insights: 4 Types of Data Analytics to Improve Decision-Making*. Harvard Business School Online. Available at: https://online.hbs.edu/blog/post/types-of-data-analysis, 2021.

CONTIPELLI, E and PICCIAU, S. *Post-COVID-19: Rebuilding Our Paradigms Through Sustainable*

Development Goals and the Sufficiency Economy Philosophy. New York: IndraStra Global, 2020.

CRADLE TO CRADLE PRODUCTS INNOVATION INSTITUTE. *Cradle to Cradle Certified*. Available at: https://c2ccertified.org/the-standard.

DANNORITZER, C et al. *The Lightbulb Conspiracy: The Untold Story of Planned Obsolescence*, San Francisco, 2011.

C40 CITIES and CLIMATE KIC. *Municipality-led circular economy: Case Studies*. Available at: https://www.climate-kic.org/wp-content/uploads/sites/15/2018/12/Municipality-led-circular-economy-case-studies-compressed-ilovepdf-compressed.pdf.

_____. *Circular Copenhagen – 70 % Waste Recycled by 2024*. Available at: https://www.c40.org/case-studies/circular-copenhagen-70-waste-recycled-by-2024/.

DÁVILA, A. O. *Economía de la innovación y del cambio tecnológico: una aproximación teórica desde el pensamiento Schumpeteriano*. Revista Ciencias Estratégicas. Vol 16 - No 20, 2008.

DELL TECHNOLOGIES, *Creating a Model for Sustainability, Dell Environmental Report*. Available at: https://i.dell.com/sites/doccontent/corporate/environment/en/documents/cr-report-2003.pdf, 2003.

_____. *Accelerating the circular economy to reduce waste and protect the planet*. https://www.dell.com/en-us/dt/corporate/social-impact/advancing-sustainability/accelerating-the-circular-economy.htm#anchor.

DEPARTMENT OF ENVIRONMENTAL QUALITY. STATE OF OREGON. *Wasted Food Measurement Study: Oregon Households*. Available at: https://www.oregon.gov/deq/mm/food/Pages/Wasted-Food-Study.aspx.

DESAI, R. *Theories of Development*. In: *Introduction to International Development: Approaches, Actors, Issues, and Practice* (43-64). Oxford University Press Canada, 2017.

DIAMOND, J. *Collapse: How Societies choose to Fail or Succeed*. London: Penguin Books, 2006.

DIMITROVA, T., ILIEVA, I., and STANEV, V. *I Consume, Therefore I Am? Hyperconsumption Behavior: Scale Development and Validation.* Social Sciences 11: 532. https://doi.org/10.3390/socsci11110532, 2022.

DYECOO. Available at: https://dyecoo.com/dyecoo/.

DOMINGUEZ, I. P., ZAMBRANO, R. E. and RODRIGUEZ, V. A. *Gen Z's Motivations towards Sustainable Fashion and Eco-Friendly Brand Attributes: The Case of Vinted.* MDPI Sustainability 15(11), Available at: https://www.mdpi.com/2071-1050/15/11/8753#B21-sustainability-15-08753, 2023.

DOUGHNUTS ECONOMICS ACTION LAB. *What is the Doughnut?* Available at: https://doughnuteconomics.org/tools-and-stories/11.

DRUCKER, P. *Innovation and Entrepreneurship: Practices and Principles.* Harper & Row, New York, 1985.

DUBEY, R. et al. *Examining the role of big data and predictive analytics on collaborative performance in context to sustainable consumption and production behaviour.* Journal of cleaner production n. 196, 1508-1521, 2018.

EKINS, P. *Economic Growth and Environmental Sustainability: the Prospects for Green Growth*, Routledge, London/New York, 2000.

ELLEN MAC ARTHUR FOUNDATION. *A New Textiles Economy: Redesigning Fashion's Future*, http://www.ellenmacarthurfoundation.org/publications, 2017.

_____. *The Plastic Pact Network.* https://ellenmacarthurfoundation.org/the-plastics-pact-network, 2023.

_____. *Circular Business Models: Rethinking business models for a thriving fashion industry.* Available at: https://www.ellenmacarthurfoundation.org/fashion-business-models/overview, 2021.

_____. *The Circular Economy Glossary.* Available at: https://www.ellenmacarthurfoundation.org/topics/circular-economy-introduction/glossary, 2021.

ELLIS, E. *A World of Our Making*. New Scientist 210 (2816): 26-27, 2011.

ENVIRONMENTAL PROTECTION AUTHORITY. *Expansion of Monkey Mia Dolphin Resort: Report and Recommendations*. Available at: https://www.epa.wa.gov.au/sites/default/files/EPA_Report/EPA%20Report%201603%20%20Expansion%20of%20the%20Monkey%20Mia%20Dolphin%20Resort.pdf.

ERGAS, H. '*Does technology policy matter?*', In: GUILE, B.R. and BROOKS, H. (eds.) *Technology and global industry: Companies and nations in the world economy*, Washington DC: National Academies Press, pp. 191-245, 1987.

EUROPEAN COMMISSION. *Internal, Market, Industry, Entrepreneurship and SMEs*. Available at: https://singleeconomy.ec.europa.eu/industry/sustainability_en#:text=Circular%20economy,Circular%20economy,again%20to%20create%20further%20value.

EUROPEAN COUNCIL. *What is the European Green Deal?* Available at: https://www.consilium.europa.eu/green-deal.

EUROSTAT. *Circular Economy: Job Creation*. Available at: https://ec.europa.eu/eurostat/tgm/refreshTableAction.do?tab=table&plugin=1&pcode=cei_cie010&language=en.

FISCHER-KOWALSKI, M. et al. *Decoupling Natural Resource Use and Environmental Impacts from Economic Growth*, UNEP, www.unep.org/resource-panel/decoupling/files/pdf/decoupling_report_english.pdf., 2011.

FOOD AND AGRICULTURE ORGANIZATION. *Food Wastage Footprint & Climate Change*. Rome: UN FAO, 2015.

FOLKE, C., et al. *Social-ecological resilience and biosphere-based sustainability science*. Ecology and Society, 21(3):41, 2016.

GALLOPIN, G. A *Systems Approach to Sustainability and Sustainable Development*. Economic Commission for Latin America, Santiago, 2003.

GANTAYAT, S.S., MISRA, A., and PANDA, B.S. *A Study of Incomplete Data – A Review*. Advances in Intelligent Systems and Computing vol. 247, Switzerland: Springer International Publishing, 2013.

GEISSDOERFER, M., MORIOKA, S. N., DE CARVALHO, M. M., & Evans, S. *Business models and supply chains for the circular economy. Journal of Cleaner Production*, 190, 712–721, 2018.

GIMENEZ, C. SIERRA, V. & RODON, J. *Sustainable Operations: Their Impact on the Triple Bottom Line*. International Journal of Production Economics, vol. 140, issue 1, 2012.

GRANSKOG, A. et al. *Biodiversity: The next frontier in sustainable fashion*. McKinsey & Company. https://www.mckinsey.com/industries/retail/ourinsights/biodiversity-the-next-frontier-in- sustainable-fashion, 2020.

GROVER, V., CHIANG, R., LIANG, T. and ZHANG, D. *Creating Strategic Business Value from Big Data Analytics: A Research Framework*. Journal of Management Information Systems 35(2): 388–423, 2018.

GULDMANN, E. *Best Practice Examples of Circular Business Models*, 2014.

GÜNTHER, W., REZAZADE MEHRIZI, M., HUYSMAN, M. and FELDBERG, F. *Debating Big data: A Literature Review on realizing Value from Big Data*, The Journal of Strategic Information Systems, 2017.

GUPTA, S., CHEN, H., HAZEN, B., KAUR, S. and SANTIBAÑEZ GONZALEZ, E. *Circular economy and big data analytics: A stakeholder perspective, Technological Forecasting and Social Change*, 2018.

HAYES, A. *What Is Greenwashing? How It Works, Examples, and Statistics*. Investopedia. Available at: https://www.investopedia.com/greenwashing, 2024.

HANSEN, S. *How Zara Grew Into the World's Largest Fashion Retailer*. The New York Times. https://www.nytimes.com/2012/11/11/magazine/how-zara-grew-into-the-worlds-largest-fashion-retailer.html, 2012.

HAWKEN, P. *The Ecology of Commerce: A Declaration of Sustainability*. Harper Collins Publishers, 1994.

HEAD, B. W. and ALFORD, J. *Wicked Problems: Implications for Public Policy and Management*, p. 101. Administration and Society. 47(6) 711-739, 2015.

H&M. *Sustainability: Circularity and Climate*. Available at: https://hmgroup.com/sustainability/circularity-and-climate/.

HUANG, M. H., RUST, R. T. *Sustainability and Consumption*. Journal of the Academy of Marketing Science 39 (1), 40–54, 2011.

IKEA. *IWAY: the IKEA Supplier Code of Conduct*. Available at: https://www.ikea.com/global/en/our-business/how-we-work/iway-our-supplier-code-of-conduct/.

JACKSON, T. *Sustainable Consumption*. In ATKINSON, G., DIETZ, S., NEUMAYER, E., Handbook of Sustainable Development, Edward Elgar Publishing, 2007.

JIN, B., CHANG, H. J. J., MATTHEWS, D. R., & GUPTA, M. Fast Fashion Business Model. *Fashion Supply Chain Management*, 193–211. https://doi.org/10.4018/978-1-60960-756-2.ch011, 1982.

JONKER et al. *The Circular Economy: Developments, Concepts, and Research in Search for Corresponding Business Models*. Nijmegen: Radboud University, 2017.

KAPTEIN, M. and VAN TULDER, R. *Toward Effective Stakeholder Dialogue*, Business and Society Review, 108:2, 203-224, 2003.

KAZA, S.; YAO, L.; BHADA-TATA, P.; VAN WOERDEN, F. *What a Waste 2.0: A Global Snapshot of Solid Waste Management to 2050*. Urban Development. Washington, DC: World Bank, 2018.

KEMP, R. and PERSON, P. *Measuring Eco-Innovation*. Report OECD, https://www.oecd.org/env/consumption-innovation/43960830.pdf, 2008.

KIM, R. and BOSSELMANN, K. *Operationalizing Sustainable Development: Ecological Integrity as a Grundnorm of International Law*. Review of European,

Comparative and International Environmental Law, July 2015.

KINGSLEY, N. *History, Principles and Concepts of Sustainability*. White World Publication, 2014.

KIRCHHERR, J., YANG, N. Nadja, SCHULZE-SPÜNTRUP, F. et al. Conceptualizing the Circular Economy (Revisited): An Analysis of 221 Definitions. Resources Conservation and Recycling, Vol. 194, 107001, 2023.

KOPNINA, H. and POLDNER, K. *Circular Economy: Challenges and Opportunities for Ethical and Sustainable Business*. Routledge, 2021.

KUBISZEWSKI et al. *Beyond GDP: Measuring and Achieving Global Genuine Progress*. In: Ecological Economics 93, 57–68, 2013.

LEELAKULTHANIT, O. *The Factors Affecting Life in Moderation*. Asian Social Science; Vol. 13, No. 1; 2017. Available at: http://dx.doi.org/10.5539/ass.v13n1p106.

LEONARD, A. *The Story of Electronics: Annotated Script* https://www.storyofstuff.org/wp-content/uploads/2020/01/SoElectronics_Annotated_Script.pdf, 2020.

LIPOVETSKY, G. *The Hyperconsumption Society*, p. 27. In Beyond Consumption Bubble. Edited by Karin Elström and Kays Glans. Routledge, 2011.

LIPPINCOTT, J. G., *Design for Business*. Chicago: P. Theobald Publishers, 1947.

LOOP INDUSTRIES. *Mission and Vision*. Available at: https://www.loopindustries.com/en/about/mission-vision.

LUNNING, F. *Fanthropologies*. University of Minnesota Press, 2010.

MASON, P. *Postcapitalism: A Guide to Our Future*. New York: Farrar, Straus and Giroux, 2016.

MARX, A and WOUTERS, J. *Is everybody on board? Voluntary sustainability standards and green restructuring*. Development (Basingstoke). https://doi.org/10.1057/s41301-016-0051-z, 2015.

MAZZUCATO, M. *The Value of Everything: Making and Taking in Global Economy*. Penguin Books, 2019.

_____. *The Entrepreneurial State: Debunking public vs. private sector myths*, p 26. Penguin Books Ltd, 2014.

_____. *Mission-oriented research & innovation in the European Union : a problem-solving approach to fuel innovation-led growth*, European Commission, Directorate-General for Research and Innovation, Publications Office, https://data.europa.eu/doi/10.2777/360325, 2018.

MC CONNELL, C. and BRUE, S. *Macroeconomics: Principles, Problems and Policies*, p. 22. New York: McGraw-Hill/Irwin, 2002.

MCDONOUGH, W. and BRAUNGART, M. *Cradle To Cradle: Remaking The Way We Make Things,* San Francisco, CA: North Point Press, 2002.

MCLEAN, L. D. *Organizational Culture's Influence on Creativity, and Innovation. A Review of the Literature and Implications for Human Resource Development*. Advances in Developing Human Resources, 7, 2005.

MEADOWS, D. H. et al. *The Limits to Growth: A Report for the Club of Rome's Project on the Predicament of Mankind.* New York: Universe Books, 1972.

MERTIG, A. & DUNLAP, R. *Environmentalism: Preservation and Conservation. In International Encyclopedia of the Social & Behavioral Sciences*, pp. 4687-4693, Pergamon, 2001.

MI, Z., COFFMAN, D. *The Sharing Economy promotes Sustainable Societies. Nat Commun* 10, 1214. Available at: https://doi.org/10.1038/s41467-019-09260-4, 2019.

MINTZBERG, H. *Structures in Fives: Designing Effective Organizations*. London: Prentice Hall, 1983.

MOATTI, S. C. *The Sharing Economy's New Middlemen. Harvard Business Review.* Available at: https://hbr.org/2015/03/the-sharing-economys-new-middlemen, 2015.

MOFFATT, I. *Sustainable Development: Principles, Analysis and Policies*. Parthenon: London, 1996.

MUD Jeans. Available at: https://mudjeans.nl, 2022.

NATH, B., HENS, L. and DEVUYST, D. *Sustainable Development*. VUB Press, 1996.

NETHERLANDS ENTERPRISE AGENCY. *Subsidy Guide*. Available at: https://english.rvo.nl/subsidy-guide.

NORDHAUS, W. *The Climate Casino: Risk, Uncertainty, and Economics for a Warming World.* New Haven: Yale University Press, 2013.

O'BRIEN, R. and WILLIAMS, M. *Global Political Economy: Evolution and Dynamics*. New York: Palgrave MacMilliam, 2004.

ONE PLANET NETWROK. *Case Studies: Innovative Greywater Recycling in Hotels: Abu Dhabi Premier Inn*. Available at: https://www.oneplanetnetwork.org/knowledge-centre/resources/innovative-greywater-recycling-hotels.

OFSTAD, S., WESTLY, L., BRATELLI, T. *Norway, Miljøverndepartementet, Symposium on Sustainable Consumption* (Eds.). Symposium: sustainable consumption: 19-20 January 1994□: Oslo,Norway. Ministry of Environment, Oslo, Norway, 1994.

ONYEAKA, H. and CHUKWUGOZIE, D. C. *Closing the Loop: How Circular Economy Approaches Can Tackle Food Waste and Promote Sustainability*. SUSTAINE.ORG, Vol. 1, Available at: https://sustaine.org/journal/index.php/sciences/, 2023.

OXFORD ADVANCE AMERICAN DICTIONARY. *Definition of Innovation*. Available at: https://www.oxfordlearnersdictionaries.com/definition/american_english/innovation.

PACKARD, V. *The Waste Makers*, David McKay Company, New York, 1960.

PARKHURST, H. B. *Confusion, lack of consensus, and the definition of creativity as a construct. Journal of Creative Behavior, 33*(1), 1-21, 1999.

PATAGONIA. *Our Environmental Responsibility Programs*. Available at: https://www.patagonia.com/our-responsibility-programs.html.

_____. *Don't Buy This Jacket*, Black Friday and the New York Times. Available at: https://www.patagonia.com/stories/dont-buy-this-jacket-black-friday-and-the-new-york-times/story-18615, 2011.

_____. *Worn Wear*. Available at: https://wornwear.patagonia.com.

PELA CASE: Our Story & Mission. Available at: https://pelacase.com/pages/our-story.

PIGNI, F. *Digital Data Streams: Creating Value from the Real-Time Flow of Big Data*, California Management Review 58: 5–25, 2016.

PIKETTY, T. *Capital in the Twenty-First Century*. Harvard University Press, 2020.

_____. *Nature, Culture, and Inequality: A Comparative Historical Perspective.* New York: Other Press, 2024.

PONGRÀCZ, E. et al. *Evolving the Theory of Waste Management: Defining key Concepts. Progress in Industrial Ecology.* An International Journal, 3, 59-74, 2004.

POPE, K. *Understanding Planned Obsolescence: Unsustainability Through Production, Consumption and Waste Generation*, Kogan Page, 2017.

PORTER, M. and KRAMER, M. R. *Creating Shared Value: How to Reinvent Capitalism—and Unleash a Wave of Innovation and Growth.* Harvard Business Review, January-February 2011.

PRAHALAD, C. K. and HART *The Fortune at the Bottom of the Pyramid.* Berkeley: Strategy+Business, issue 26. Available at: https://people.eecs.berkeley.edu/Fortune-BoP, 2002.

PRESTON, F. *A Global Redesign? Shaping the Circular Economy.* Chantam House: Briefing Paper, 2012.

PROCIRC. Pilot Projects: *Attractive refurbished furniture in Government of Flanders' offices*. Available at: https://northsearegion.eu/procirc/pilot-projects/attractive-refurbished-furniture-in-government-of-flanders-offices/.

RADJOU, N. and PRABHU, J. *Frugal Innovation: How to Do Better with Less*. Economist Book, 2015.

RAWORTH, K. *Doughnut Economics: Seven Ways to Think Like a 21st-Century Economist*. London: Penguin Books, 2022.

REMY, N. et al. *Style that's sustainable: A new fast-fashion formula*. McKinsey & Company https://www.mckinsey.com/capabilities/sustainability/our-insights/style-thats-sustainable-a-new-fast-fashion-formula, 2020.

RITTEL, H. W. J. and WEBBER, M. M. *Dilemmas in a General Theory of Planning. Political Sciences*. 4, 155-169, 1973.

ROSTOV, W. W. *The Stages of Economic Growth: A Non-Communist Manifesto*. Cambridge University Press, 1991.

SAGIROGLU, S. *Big data: A Review*. 2013 International Conference on Collaboration Technologies and Systems (CTS). pp. 42–47, 2013.

SAHAN, E. et all. *What Doughnuts Economics means for Business: Creating Enterprises that are Regenerative and Distributive by Design*. Doughnuts Economics Action Lab.

SCHENKEL et al. *Understanding value creation in closed loop supply chains: Past findings and future directions. Journal of Manufacturing Systems*, *37*(3), 729-745, 2015.

SCHÖNBERG, H. *Creating value with data in circular business models of textiles*. Available at: https://aaltodoc.aalto.fi/items/6ae10fee-bcc8-42cd-ac41-12bea33ffb89, 2022.

SCHUMACHER, E. F., *Small is Beatiful: A Study of Economics as if People Mattered*. London: Abacus, 1990.

SCHUMPETER, J. A. *The Theory of Economic Development: An Inquiry into Profits, Capital, Credit, Interest and the Business Cycle*, New Brunswick (U.S.A) and London (U.K.): Transaction Publishers, 1934.

_____. *Capitalism, Socialism and Democracy*, HarperCollins, 1968 (2008).

SKOTTSBERG, C. *The Natural History of Juan Fernandez and Easter Island 1*. Uppsala, Sweden: Almqvist & Wiksells Boktryckeri, 1956.

SMITH, G. *Better World Books: A Case Study in Sustainability*. Available at: https://www.gregoryasmith.info/better-world-books, 2020.

SOULE, S. A., MALHORTRA, N. and CLAVIER, B., *Defining Social Innovation, Stanford GSB*, https://www.gsb.stanford.edu/experience/about/centers-institutes/csi/defining-social-innovation.

STOCKHOLM RESILIENCE CENTRE. *All planetary boundaries mapped out for the first time*. https://www.stockholmresilience.org/5.3d04209a18a2642b2fc162a3.html.

THAILAND SUSTAINABLE DEVELOPMENT FOUNDATION. *Sufficiency for Sustainability*. Available at: http://tsdf.nida.ac.th/en/, 2018.

TARDI, C. *Animal Spirits: Meaning, Definition in Finance, and Examples*. Investopedia. Available at: https://www.investopedia.com/terms/a/animal-spirits.asp, 2023.

TEKINER, F. and KEANE, J. *Big Data Framework*. IEEE International Conference on Systems, Man, and Cybernetics, Available at: https://ieeexplore.ieee.org/document/6722011, 2013.

TOAST ALE. *Sustainability*. Available at: https://www.toastbrewing.com/sustainability.

TONY'S CHOCOLONELY. *Tony's Open Chain*. Available at: https://www.tonysopenchain.com/our-approach/tonys-5-sourcing-principles.

TOOZE, A. *Welcome to the World of the Polycrisis*. Financial Times n. 28, 2022.

TOO GOOD TO GO. Available at: https://www.toogoodtogo.com/en-ca, 2023.

TUCCI, L. & LASKOWSKI, N. *Definition: Sharing Economy*. Available at: https://www.techtarget.com/sharing-economy, 2018.

UNITED NATIONS *Transforming our world: the 2030 Agenda for Sustainable Development*. https://sustainabledevelopment.un.org/post2015/transformingourworld, 2015.

_____. *Glossary of Environment Statistics*, Studies in Methods, Series F, No. 67, New York, 1997.

_____. *Report of the World Commission on Environment and Development: Our Common Future*, 1987.

UNITED NATIONS DEVELOPMENT PROGRAMME. *The Climate Dictionary: Speak Climate Fluently*. New York: UNDP, 2023.

UNITED NATIONS ENVIRONMENTAL PROGRAMME. *Putting the brakes on fast fashion*. https://www.unep.org/news-and-stories/story/putting-brakes-fast-fashion, 2018.

_____. *Sustainable Lifestyles, Cities and Industry*. Available at: http://www.oneearthweb.org/communicating-sustainable-lifestyles-report.html.

UNITED NATIONS FORUM ON SUSTAINABILITY STANDARDS. *1st Flagship Report of the United Nations Forum on Sustainability Standards (UNFSS)*. Available at: https://unfss. org/home/flagship-publication/, 2013.

UNITED NATIONS WORLD TOURISM ORGANIZATION. *Definition of Sustainable Tourism*. Available at: https://www.unwto.org/sustainable-development.

_____. *The One Planet Sustainable Tourism Program*. Available at: https://www.unwto.org/sustainable-development/one-planet.

VINTED. *About us*. Available at: https://www.vinted.com/about, 2024.

WANG, L. et al. *IoT-Enabled Real-time Energy Efficiency Optimization Method for Energy-Intensive Manufacturing Enterprises*. International Journal of Computer Integrated Manufacturing, 31(4-5), 362-379, 2018.

_____. and ALEXANDER, C. A. *Big Data Driven Supply Chain Management and Business Administration*.

American Journal of Economics and Business Administration, 7 (2): 60-67, 2015.

WEETMAN, C. *A Circular Economy Handbook: How to Build a More Resilient, Competitive and Sustainable Business*. Kogan Page, 2020.

WILLIS, K. *Theories and Practices of Development*. Routledge perspectives on development. Routledge. http://site.ebrary.com/lib/alltitles/docDetail.action?docID=10462497, 2011.

WHITEHEAD LOTH, S. *5 Truths the fast fashion industry doesn't want you to know*. Huffington Post. https://www.huffpost.com/entry/5-truths-the-fast-fashion_b_5690575, 2014.

WORLD BANK. *World Development Report 2003: Sustainable Development in a Dynamic World--Transforming Institutions, Growth, and Quality of Life*. Available at: http://hdl.handle.net/10986/5985, 2003.

_____. *World Development Report 2006: Equity and Development*. New York: A copublication of The World Bank and Oxford University Press, 2006.

_____. *World Development Report 2021: Data for Better Lives*. Washington: International Bank for Reconstruction and Development/The World Bank. Available at: https://www.worldbank.org/en/wdr2021.

_____. *Squaring the Circle: Policies from Europe's Circular Economy Transition*, https://documents1.worldbank.org/curated/en/099425006222229520/pdf/P174596025fa8105a091c50fb22f0596fd1.pdf, 2022.

WORLD BUSINESS COUNCIL FOR SUSTAINABLE DEVELOPMENT (WBCSD). *Food Loss and Waste Accounting and Reporting Standard* .Available at: https://www.wbcsd.org/resources/food-loss-and-waste-accounting-and-reporting-standard-2/.

WORLD ECONOMIC FORUM. *Open Up a Sustainable Wardrobe*. Available at: https://wef.ch/353dYI7 #sdi19 #sustainableworld.

VAN TULDER, R. *Business & The Sustainable Development Goals: A Framework for Effective Corporate Involvement*. Rotterdam School of Management, Erasmus University, Rotterdam, 2018.

VELENTURF, A. P., and PURNELL, P. Principles for a sustainable circular economy. *Sustainable Production and Consumption*, 27, p. 1437-1457, 2021.

VEJA. *Production | VEJA*, https://project.veja-store.com/en/single/production, 2021.

VERGRAGT, P.J. et al. *Fostering and Communicating Sustainable Lifestyles: Principles and Emerging Practices*,

ZALASIEWICZ, J. *The Human Dimension in Geological Time*. In: MÖLLERS et all. *Welcome to the Anthropocene: The Earth in Our Hands*. Munich: Rachel Carson Center, 2014.

ZHU et al. *Confirmation of a Measurement Model for Green Supply Chain Management Practices Implementation*. In: International Journal of Production Economics 111(2), 2010.

www.ingramcontent.com/pod-product-compliance
Lightning Source LLC
Chambersburg PA
CBHW052148220526
45471CB00004B/1586